24 HOURS IN
ANCIENT
ATHENS

Also in this series:

24 HOURS IN ANCIENT ATHENS

A DAY IN THE LIFE OF THE PEOPLE WHO LIVED THERE

PHILIP MATYSZAK

Michael O'Mara Books Limited

This paperback edition first published in 2021

First published in Great Britain in 2019 by
Michael O'Mara Books Limited
9 Lion Yard
Tremadoc Road
London SW4 7NQ

A CIP catalogue record for this book is
available from the British Library.

Papers used by Michael O'Mara Books Limited are natural,
recyclable products made from wood grown in sustainable forests.
The manufacturing processes conform to the environmental
regulations of the country of origin.

ISBN: 978-1-78929-350-0 in paperback print format
ISBN: 978-1-78243-977-6 in ebook format

1 2 3 4 5 6 7 8 9 10

Designed and typeset by Ed Pickford
Cover design and illustration © Patrick Knowles
Printed and bound by CPI Group (UK) Ltd, Croydon, CR0 4YY

www.mombooks.com

To T.P., the Dancing Queen of Crossgates.

CONTENTS

INTRODUCTION

Welcome to Athens in 416 BC. The month is Elaphebolion, just before the theatrical festival of the Great Dionysia (early April). At this time, the urban population of Athens is around 30,000, with a greater concentration of geniuses per square foot than at any other time in human history.

As the city hovers on the brink of the fateful war that will destroy its golden age, we spend twenty-four hours with regular Athenians who occasionally encounter some of the city's great men – not as paragons of intellectual ability but as people with very human concerns. After all, geniuses spend little time being geniuses. Mostly they are normal people who go to the bathroom, argue with their spouses and enjoy a drink with friends.

In most ancient texts we meet the ordinary people of Athens only when they interact with the city's exceptional characters. This book turns this around, so that we only meet the geniuses of Athens when they interact with ordinary citizens going about their daily business.

Where a chapter of this book is not based on archaeological reconstruction, it is usually a contemporary text repackaged and presented from the perspective of an ordinary Athenian. Where a chapter has thus been rewritten, I have indicated where the original is to be found.

Some of the reconstructions are speculative, although based on the best research now available. Every hour of a day in the life of these Athenians is designed to capture – preferably in the very words of those same Athenians – their experience of living in this extraordinary, dynamic, brilliant and amoral city at the very peak of its greatness.

Today, in the spring of 416, Athens is enjoying an interlude of peace in the devastating Peloponnesian War of 431 to 404 BC. The first round of warfare came to an end with the Peace of Nicias, five years previously. Despite repeated Spartan attacks, which devastated the city's farms and orchards, Athens came out of that war stronger than ever. In fact, now goaded by Alcibiades, the *enfant terrible* of Athenian politics, the city is contemplating the audacious invasion and conquest of Sicily.

In this frenetic atmosphere of epoch-changing innovation and political intrigue, where some of the greatest works of western civilization are being forged with the tools of slavery and imperial oppression, ordinary Athenians are trying to get on with their everyday lives in extraordinary circumstances.

This is their story.

THE TEMPLE GUARD REMEMBERS

There are few atheists in Athens. Those few might change their minds if they also changed places with Pentarkes the Elean. Pentarkes is on night watch in the very heart of the Acropolis, within the Parthenon of Athena. At midnight Pentarkes is very well aware of that goddess. She is standing behind him right now.

The flickering light of the oil lamps casts the shadow of the goddess before him, so that her ornate helmet moves slightly – as if Athena tilts her head as she considers this mortal in her domain. Pentarkes is sure that her eyes, lapis lazuli blue in daylight, are now their true colour – the steel-grey of the Athenian sky just before dawn. They call her 'the grey-eyed goddess': sacred Athena, daughter of wisdom, goddess of the battleline.

Pentarkes turns slowly so that he first sees the goddess by her reflection in the iridescent pool of oil at her feet. Without looking up to see, he knows she is tall, nine times the height of a man, and her skin is ivory-white. A pale arm reaches out, as though offering victory as a prize. Literally so, for the goddess has transferred her golden spear to rest against her shoulder so that Nike, the embodiment of Victory, can perch on her palm.

Victory is a fickle thing, which can at any moment fly away on gilded wings, so it is reassuring to know that Athena remains forever protecting her city. Like any respectable Athenian woman, the goddess wears a *peplos*, a garment that hangs from the shoulder and is girdled at the waist before it falls elegantly to her ankles. A commoner's *peplos* is plain, unbleached wool. An aristocratic lady might flaunt a *peplos* of purple linen. Only Athena, favourite of Zeus and companion of heroes, wears a *peplos* of pure gold.

Pentarkes steps back, the better to see the face of his goddess. She looks unusually serious tonight. Is she thinking of that day, half a lifetime ago, when she was brought to life by the hand of a genius? The divine Athena was born from the head of Zeus but the body she now inhabits, the awe-inspiring statue in this temple made specially to house her, was made by Pheidias, the greatest sculptor not just of this, but (in the highly biased opinion of Pentarkes) any other age.

The statues of Pheidias are the most perfect of their kind that has ever been seen.

CICERO *DE ORATORE* 2.9

Much has happened since then. But Athena remains – majestic, yet somehow approachable, magnificent in daylight, but only truly alive in the lamplight when she stands guard alongside Pentarkes.

Pentarkes first met Pheidias almost seventeen years ago, in Elis, a small city in the Peloponnese. Even as a lad

Pentarkes enjoyed a certain distinction as an athlete, and was consequently welcomed into the workshop of the master sculptor. To carve the likeness of the great gods of Greece, Pheidias explained, was a privilege allowed to only a few. In Elis, the Athenian sculptor had been commissioned to produce a masterwork – a statue of the patron of the Olympic games, mighty Zeus himself. (At this time, the city of Elis was in charge of organizing the Olympics.)

Pentarkes remembers Pheidias striding back and forth in a dusty workshop littered with samples of marble, ivory and rare cedar wood. Forgetting his young visitor, Pheidias mutters to himself. 'At the moment he passes judgement on a matter of grave importance, that's when to show him. Grave, austere, terrifying in his majesty. Yes!' He quotes from the *Iliad*:

> *The son of Cronus speaks, dipping his head and dark brow,*
> *and the anointed hair of the great god*
> *falls back from his divine head*
> *as Olympus is shaken!* [1]

'That's it! Homer had it right. He will be sitting on his throne, and I shall make him as I did Athena, splendid in gold and ivory. On his head, a crown – no, a garland. I shall make the garland as if of shoots of the olive tree – because Athena, Goddess of the Olive, came from those very brows on which the garland rests.

'To the Olympic champions goes the victory so I shall show him also holding Nike (Athena won't mind, I hope). In the other hand of Zeus, a sceptre. I'll push the committee for funds to encrust the sceptre with every kind of jewel. Atop the sceptre, well, it must be an eagle. Gold! The robe must be gold, embroidered with figures of animals, and flowers. Lilies I think. Lilies carve well.'

Lilies carved well, indeed. Twelve years after its first showing to the astonished and delighted populace of Olympia, the statue of Zeus at Olympia is now considered one of the wonders of the known world, along with the Great Pyramid at Giza and the Hanging Gardens of Babylon. Yet the people of Elis owe their masterpiece to Athens. Not to the greatness of Athens, but to Athens at its worst – with its petty jealousy, back-stabbing and rabble-rousing politicians.

Pheidias seems to me the only artist to truly portray Olympian Zeus. I came to see his statue with high expectations, but he far surpassed them.

L. AEMILIUS PAULLUS, CONQUEROR OF MACEDON,
POLYBIUS *HISTORIES* 30.10

Pheidias was still a lad then, and the Persian Wars not long over. Much of Athens was still in ruins after the Persian army had occupied the city in 480 BC and done their best to wreck the place. Persian wrath had focused on the Acropolis. The fire-worshipping Persians had little use for a temple of Athena and had demolished it.

Pericles led the Athenian democracy not through any rank or elected office, but simply by the sheer strength of his personality. He decided that the Acropolis and particularly the temple of Athena would be rebuilt, and rebuilt to out-do any other building in the world. Only the best materials would be used for the new temple. The walls would be of Pentelic marble, the roof of cedar beams and gilded tiles.

The Golden Ratio

Divide a line into two parts in such a way that the long part divided by the smaller part has the same ratio as the whole line divided by the longer part. The ratio of the longer line to the shorter line is 1.618… (As with pi the digits have no end.)

The Golden Ratio is used in both art and engineering and therefore in architecture, which is art and engineering combined. The length to width of the Parthenon fits the Golden Ratio, which is no surprise as the person who discovered this ratio was Pheidias. In mathematical equations the ratio is symbolized by the Greek letter phi (Φ) – the opening letter of Pheidias' name.

The lesser statues would be marble from the island of Paros, the finest in the known world. The statue of Athena would be the centrepiece of the temple that would be the core of the Acropolis, as the Acropolis is the heart of Athens. For such a statue, marble was inadequate. This statue would be of polished ivory and pure gold and, in the majesty of Athena, worshippers would see the majesty of Athena's city and people.

A committee of three oversaw the construction. One procured the workers and materials, another was in charge of architecture and engineering, and a third had the task of blending all the elements into a single artistic whole. That third man was Pheidias.

No one denies that Pheidias and his colleagues did a superb job. In a moment of vanity, however, Pheidias indulged himself and his sponsor Pericles. In a frieze depicting Athenians and

Amazons in battle he carved himself as a warrior hurling a stone at the enemy and added a very fine likeness of Pericles in battle with an Amazon. Even worse, there were rumours that Pheidias invited well-born women allegedly to view the works in progress, while really making them available for Pericles to seduce.

The enemies of Pericles decided that they could harm him by taking down Pheidias. Accordingly, an employee of the sculptor was persuaded to testify that Pheidias had helped himself to the gold allocated for Athena's garments.

This was a lot of gold, for the statue of Athena Parthenos was not intended merely as the glory of Athens, but also as the city's reserve bank. The gold from the goddess' robe could be removed in an emergency and to pay for ships and men – provided it was afterwards replaced. In fact, the *cella* – the room where the statue was housed – had one unusual feature. Unlike the same room in most temples, this one was divided in two. The second, very secure room behind the goddess was a storehouse containing gold, silver and the tribute from subject cities of the Athenian empire.

Pericles had foreseen both the risk of embezzlement and the political possibility of that accusation. Accordingly, he had ordered Pheidias to make sure that the golden clothes of the goddess could be removed and weighed if needed. This was done, and it was demonstrated that all the gold was present and accounted for. 'Ah,' said Pheidias' treacherous assistant. 'Did I say gold? I meant ivory. He embezzled some of the ivory from which the statue was made.' The ivory was an integral part of the statue and could not be removed and weighed. Unable to prove himself innocent, Pheidias was promptly found guilty and hauled off to prison.

Pentarkes never discovered how Pheidias had got out of an Athenian prison to reach Elis in the Peloponnese, nor

**PHEIDIAS DISPLAYS A MODEL OF HIS EPIC STATUE OF
ATHENA TO THE COMMITTEE**

how he had thereafter become chief designer for the statue of
Zeus. Almost certainly the hand of Pericles was behind this
manoeuvre, possibly because even after the abrupt departure of
Pheidias, work on the Parthenon still had to go ahead.

This meant that Pheidias was still needed. He had left
in Athens a school of young artists who had taken up the
challenge of finishing what their master had begun. Pentarkes
remembers how every day, often at inappropriate moments,
messengers from Athens would pop into the studio at Elis.
There were questions about the proportions of different
statues, how they should be aligned, the type of stone to be
used for the pediments and thousands of other minor details.
Over time, listening to the project as it developed, Pentarkes
became almost as obsessed with the Parthenon as Pheidias
still was. He must behold for himself this epic building and

that dramatic statue of Athena that had so nearly been the ruin of his master. He was overwhelmed by curiosity as to how all the little details about which he had heard so much had turned out in reality.

Pheidias gave his student permission to go, but he did it with great reluctance. Over time he and Pentarkes had become lovers. Later, Pentarkes discovered that Pheidias had repeated his indulgences with the statue of Athena with his statue of Zeus. The youth receiving a prize at the base of the statue is Pentarkes.

Abraham Zeus Lincoln

Those interested in what the statue of Zeus might have looked like should visit one of the many pseudo-Greek temples in Washington, DC. (The early Americans knew their classics.) The Lincoln Memorial, with its friezes and Doric marble columns, houses a statue of Lincoln sitting on a throne-like chair in a conscious imitation of what Olympian Zeus might have looked like (though at just short of 6 metres high, this is half the height of the Pheidias statue of Zeus). And yes, the building in which the statue is housed is close to Pheidias' Golden Ratio at 57.8 by 36.1 metres.

Some users of sign language believe that, rather like Pheidias, the sculptor of the Lincoln statue could not resist adding a hidden message. The fingers of the seated Lincoln allegedly read 'A. L.' in sign language, possibly for the benefit of the sculptor's son who was deaf.

What to say of Athens? For a young man from a rural town, the place was overwhelming. It was exhilarating to push through the crowds in the Agora, hearing the accents of Syracuse and Persia mingling with the barbarous mutterings of near-naked Thracian slaves. In Elis, the last citizen was abed soon after sundown; in Athens, parties continued by torchlight late into the night. Street artists and acrobats performed, while philosophers debated the meaning of reality in a stoa only a few yards away.

Pentarkes believes that he became an Athenian the moment his ship nosed into the Piraeus. The port of Athens was packed with ships, from tubby little local fishing boats to hulking merchantmen and lean, shark-like triremes that glided by into the inner harbour. He could not take his eyes from the bustle and the air of purposeful chaos.

Later, he came to understand that this was not just the dominating mood of the Piraeus, but of the whole city. The people of Athens might not know where their city was going or how they were going to get there but nevertheless they were going there – faster and more stylishly than any people ever had before. It was a time when anything seemed possible.

Pentarkes rented an upper room in the tavern of Phanagora and Demetrios, near the Temple of Zeus on the road from the Piraeus to Athens. By day he wandered the Acropolis, trading on his acquaintance with Pheidias to be admitted to the cliques of sculptors, painters and stonemasons who swarmed over the site. As they worked, the most beautiful building in the world was taking shape right before his eyes. How could Pentarkes leave?

In the late afternoons and evenings, Pentarkes would stretch his allowance by helping out in the tavern downstairs. As he worked he enthused to all who would listen about the vistas and spectacles of the Parthenon. He found an all-too-ready audience in Celandine, the innkeeper's daughter. Celandine is a beautiful yellow wild flower, and Pentarkes found the flower's namesake beautiful also.

In time, Celandine became more formally known as 'Celandine, wife of Pentarkes the Elean', and Pentarkes began learning the business of tavern-keeping from his mother-in-law.

Pentarkes became an Athenian. Well, properly speaking, he became a metic. The only way to become a full Athenian citizen is to be born in Athens of Athenian parents. 'You can no more become an Athenian than a cat can become a dog,' the saying goes. Being a metic, however, is close enough. 'Metic' is short for *metoikos* – literally a 'changer of dwelling-place'. Athens might guard its citizenship jealously, but it cannot do without its metics. There are tens of thousands of them – merchants, clerks, priests, sailors and, yes, tavernkeepers.

Pure-blood Athenians affect to sneer at resident foreigners, but the metics bear the sneers quite equably, since they are often considerably richer than the Athenians doing the sneering. Many Athenians are farmers, and owning agricultural property is forbidden to foreigners. If these Athenians knew how often the metics refer to them as 'hayseeds' behind their backs they might feel somewhat less superior.

Metics drive the complex engine of the Athenian economy, and their taxes help to power the triremes of the Athenian fleet that dominates the sea. (Metics pay an extra tax for the privilege of living in Athens.) Since Pentarkes the assistant tavernkeeper is earning considerably more in Athens than Pentarkes the minor landowner would do in Elis, he accepts his lower status without regret. He has now a healthy son and a plump, pretty daughter, both of whom will also be metics, though they have never known any home but Athens.

As a metic, Pentarkes cannot attend the Assembly (an exclusion he shares with Athenian women and slaves) and he cannot serve as a juror. He can certainly prosecute a case in the Athenian courts, and in fact recently did so when a supplier sold him several kegs of vinegar that he was passing off as wine. Pentarkes remembers the expression of the jurors as they passed around a beaker of the stuff before they awarded him a full refund – with damages.

Though he can't attend the Assembly, Pentarkes is affected by its decrees. Metics serve in the Athenian army and train as thoroughly as any citizen. Pentarkes is wealthy enough to afford a panoply – that set of armour and weaponry which makes him a full hoplite, the top class of Athenian warrior. If Athens goes to war then, willing or not, Pentarkes will fight alongside the men who voted for it.

During the recent war with Sparta, Pentarkes served in Thrace, and so missed the devastating plague of Athens, which killed his beloved Celandine. (The tavern was run in his absence by Phanagora, his mother-in-law, who is apparently indestructible.) Now the metic Pentarkes is a trusted servant of Athens. No one doubts his loyalty or his fitness to do his duty to the city by serving on the Acropolis guard, even within the very heart of the temple of Athena.

The scuff of sandals on stone tells Pentarkes that his relief is on the way. His watch is nearly done. Soon others will take his place beside the goddess, though who is guarding whom, Pentarkes cannot really say. He will enter the guard house, exchange a crude joke or two with his fellow guards, then gulp a mug of cheap wine before a few hours' sleep prior to the early morning watch.

Then he will stand guard again as the dawn colours that steel-grey sky, and the first tiny figures fill the Agora below. He will stop in the temple before he goes off duty and salute his Lady once more. Then it's down the long steps, through the various checkpoints on his way to the lower city, and the walk between the Long Walls home to the tavern.

Sometimes he wonders what became of Pheidias. At some point during the war with Sparta, Pheidias seems to have slipped away from hostile Elis and no one knows what became of him. His genius has vanished from the world for ever. What would Pheidias make of Pentarkes if the master sculptor could see his lover now, with his receding hairline and face tanned to leather by long summer campaigns?

Pheidias is the most famous sculptor of any nation … and he is rightly praised.

PLINY THE ELDER *NATURAL HISTORY* 36.18

No one, seeing the seasoned warrior in his armour, or the jovial innkeeper exchanging jokes with his patrons, would associate him with the lean, golden boy from Elis. Yet on the little finger of Zeus, as he sits in his majesty at Olympia, on the very finger of the King of the Gods, Pheidias has carved a name. *Pentarkes Kalos*, it says. 'Pentarkes the Beautiful'.

Yes, Pentarkes thinks. Beneath his breastplate he pulls in the stubborn paunch that gets unstoppably larger every year. Then, I *was* beautiful.

Pheidias

Pheidias steps into the historical record when Pericles entrusted him with the artistic aspect of major projects in Athens in around 450 BC. Pheidias is credited with creating the 'high classical' style of sculpture. This shows men and women in their prime, physically perfect with remote, serene expressions. Naturally this works best with depictions of the Greek gods. (When we say, 'he has the body of a Greek god', it is the gods of Pheidias whom we invoke.)

Most of what we know of Pheidias comes from Plutarch, who wrote over half a millennium later. The exact circumstances of Pheidias' exile are impossibly murky but, according to Plato, once he was in Elis, Pheidias' skills were eagerly sought and he became remarkably wealthy (Plato *Meno* 91D). It is generally agreed Pheidias' death was unpleasant, though whether this was at the hands of the Athenians, Eleans or Spartans remains unclear.

THE SLAVES
GET PLAYFUL

Technically, Dareia is in the *andron* – a part of the house reserved for males. Usually the master of the house entertains guests here. But it is clear that this room has no such purpose. The dim light of a single oil lamp shows little more than a writing desk, but in the shadows the usual couches have been pushed against the wall, and scrolls, clothing and a half-eaten roll of bread with olives occupy the seats.

Furthermore, the only other occupant of this man's domain is also female. Their hair spilling off their necks, the two study the contents of the desk. Suddenly, Dareia's companion speaks in dramatic tones.

'Ah, Lampito. You dear Spartan girl with your delightful face, scrubbed in the rosy spring! You stride so easily, sleek and slender, yet look as if you could strangle a bull.'

In reply, Dareia makes a spirited attempt at reproducing the broad vowels of the Spartan accent, but is uncomfortably aware that it sounds more as though she has a throat cold. The Spartans are a reclusive people, and the few from Laconia who turn up in Athens are remarkably, well, laconic, so it's not as if she has heard a lot of material to imitate.

She studies the scroll before her. How, she wonders, do you scrub your face in a rosy spring? Yet 'rosy' is what the playwright has written. He actually crossed it out and then put it back again.

Her companion Chryseis sighs impatiently and resumes her part in the play. '"What lovely breasts you own!"'

Dareia rears back from the groping hands of Chryseis, who remarks defensively, 'It's what the script says – look, you're meant to reply, "Ooh, your fingers assess them with such tickles and tender chucks. It makes me feel like a victim at the altar."'

Is this, Dareia wonders, meant to be funny? Then she remembers that on an Athenian stage the lines and actions will be delivered by male actors (women are played by men in Athenian theatre). So yes, the sight of two men in drag affectionately fondling a set of fake breasts on stage is exactly the sort of bawdy humour for which the playwright – her owner Aristophanes – is notorious.

Dareia knows that she and Chryseis are unusual slave girls because both can read. That's an achievement of which many a freeborn Athenian girl cannot boast, but not perhaps altogether surprising in servants of the leading comic playwright in Athens. The playwright, Aristophanes, has just retired to bed, leaving an ink-spotted draft of his latest comedy for an early enactment by the enterprising pair.

Chryseis studies her character's name. 'Lysistrata. That's uncommon. Not many people call their daughters "Stand down the army". What's wrong with Neaira – "Newly arisen"? Or Eudokia – "Good-looking"?'

'Well, you're giving hostages to fortune with names like

that. There's Ekaterina – "Purity" – that girl from the Eudoxus household, the one who has a dozen boyfriends. Look at me. My name means "rich in possessions" and I don't even own this tunic on my back. And you're Chryseis …' Dareia stops, embarrassed.

Chryseis' name is a sore point. One can come to be a slave in Athens in many different ways. Chryseis has told Dareia that her journey started twenty-five years ago when Lycian pirates captured a boat near Halicarnassus. On the boat was Chryseis' mother, the daughter of a minor aristocrat. That aristocratic father declined to pay the pirates' ransom, so his daughter was sold into slavery. (The father had two other daughters, each expecting an expensive dowry, which might have affected his decision.) So Chryseis was born while her mother was a concubine to a minor Persian administrator in Anatolia.

'Golden' her name might mean, but Chryseis is as swarthy as her Persian father. Captured in a Greek raid on the coastal town where she lived, Chryseis at age eighteen was sold in Athens as part of the booty of that raid. She had been taught to read and write by her mother. This attracted the playwright Aristophanes, who needed a slave secretary, cleaner and general factotum. Chryseis has been in the playwright's household ever since.

At least Chryseis knows who her father was. Dareia doesn't. She got her name from her ambitious mother. That mother was a slave prostitute in one of the better-class brothels in the Kydathenaion (the largest of the five administrative areas within the city of Athens itself). Not wanting her daughter to follow the family profession, Dareia's mother had one way or another managed not only to ensure her child was literate, but also that she was familiar with basic accountancy. Then Dareia was sold to one of the brothel's regular patrons – Aristophanes. Once Dareia had joined the household, Chryseis, partly out of boredom, had completed the girl's education.

It is not a bad existence. Both girls have been slaves all their lives, and regard themselves as well above some of the freeborn poor whom they regularly see begging in the gutter. At least they are fed and clothed and have a warm bed to sleep in at night.

Furthermore, slavery is seen by most Greeks as a form of severe social disadvantage rather than as an inherent genetic

THALIA, THE MUSE OF COMEDY, HOLDING
A COMIC MASK

trait. (Among fellow Greeks, that is. Everyone knows that barbarians are born to be slaves.) Well-educated Greek slaves regard their condition as temporary, as do their owners. Certainly neither Dareia nor Chryseis intends to die in servitude. Chryseis is being courted by one of the retainers of a Phoenician merchant, a boy who finds her copper skin and dark curls highly attractive. If Aristophanes sells her, Chryseis will marry him and demand her freedom as her dowry. After that, anything is possible.

Dareia is aiming for Aristophanes himself. Well, why not? Many a concubine has seamlessly made the transition to wife. Aristophanes is in his early thirties, which is just the right age to marry. Athenian men tend to take wives ten to fifteen years younger than themselves, so he and seventeen-year-old Dareia are well-matched. Why should he wed some gawky aristocratic girl he barely knows?

Aristophanes has no need to marry into money, and he cares little for the political elite of Athens whom he regularly skewers in his plays. A few years back the populist politician Kleon was so outraged by how he was portrayed in one of Aristophanes' comedies that he dragged the playwright into court. (Despite this – or perhaps because of it – the play won first prize at the Lenaia festival that year. Athenians certainly do not venerate their leaders.)

Kleon's outrage may have been because Aristophanes subtly hinted that the politician was dishonest. Dareia remembers reading the exact words:

This villain, this bare-faced thief, this villain, this villain – I can't say the word often enough, because he acts the villain a thousand times a day. Strike him, throw him down and crush him to pieces, hate him …

You shake out the treasury like a ripe fig tree ... you know how to extort those guileless citizens, meek as lambs, yet wealthy and scared of lawsuits.[2]

Although Kleon was not Aristophanes' greatest fan, oddly enough, Socrates and Aristophanes get along amiably. This says a lot about Socrates, because few relationships could survive the treatment that Aristophanes gave Socrates in *The Clouds*. It is not often that a philosopher has an entire comic play dedicated to him alone, and that play was a merciless send-up of Socrates, his character and his ideas (ideas Aristophanes portrayed as manufactured in a sort of workshop called the 'Thinkery'). This was one of Aristophanes' less successful plays.

As the Athenian gossip machine later revealed to Dareia, Socrates himself was responsible for that. Instead of wincing or getting outraged at the well-aimed barbs, the philosopher showed every sign of genuinely enjoying the proceedings. The theatrical festival of the Dionysia attracts hordes of foreigners to the city, and when some of these puzzled spectators at the play asked, 'Who is this Socrates fellow?' the fellow in question stood up and cheerfully waved to the audience by way of introduction.

Instead of applauding the deflation of a self-important egomaniac, the audience decided that Aristophanes was victimizing an obviously well-grounded and good-natured individual who also happened to be known as something of a war hero. (When taking a break from debating ethics or the nature of the soul, Socrates in battle fights like a rabid wolf.) Aristophanes' play came third – in a field of three.

Dareia definitely approves of *The Clouds*. One of the leading characters, Strepsiades, is struggling with debt

Aristophanes

Aristophanes is considered the greatest writer in the school of 'Old Comedy' in Athens, although he had the considerable advantage that he was the only playwright of the school whose plays survive (we have eleven of his forty or so productions).

Aristophanes was never a struggling playwright starving in a garret. He was from a wealthy family (they seem to have owned property on the island of Aegina) and enjoyed an extremely good education. He was something of a scholar of Homer's works and was well capable of holding his own while among the leading philosophers of his day.

Aristophanes was a relentless opponent of war, and *Lysistrata* is but one of the plays in which he bitterly castigates the futility of war and the stupidity of those who drag his city into it.

We do not know whom Aristophanes eventually married, but marry he did, for one of his three sons seems to have finished and staged two of the plays that were incomplete when Aristophanes died some time around 386 BC.

because his spoiled aristocratic wife allows their equally spoiled son to spend the fortune that Strepsiades has not got. Dareia is in total agreement that aristocratic wives are a bad idea; women who over-indulge in horses, silks and fast living. Aristophanes needs someone good looking, with experience in household affairs and who is sensible yet stylish. To find this someone, Aristophanes need not look further than the pillow beside his on the bed. Dareia doggedly perseveres with her matrimonial project, though for someone who has made a career out of working with words, Aristophanes seems amazingly blind to even the most unsubtle hints.

After a brief and rather tense silence, the slaves resume reading the script of *Lysistrata*. Through unspoken agreement they've stopped playing the different parts for the moment. Eventually Chryseis remarks, 'Oh, it seems that we are giving up sex.'

Dareia pauses, being much further up the scroll from Chryseis. 'Why? On religious grounds?'

'In a way. All the women of Greece swear an oath not to do it. Here, at these lines, "Not on my back staring at the ceiling, nor on my hands and knees doing the Lion on the cheesegrater." It's total abstinence.'

'That leaves other alternatives,' remarks Dareia with professional interest, 'For instance ...'

She pauses, suddenly struck by the implications of the text. One does not write an anti-war play for no reason. So the rumours at the market are true. The peace is breaking.

While Dareia likes the idea of Lysistrata calling a meeting to get the women of Greece to keep their knees together until the men stop fighting, she's sure there would be fighting anyway. There is always fighting. Recently the Athenians were fighting in Egypt – that went badly, yet even so Athens had to launch into another war in Asia Minor, which is how Chryseis ended up in Athens. Then the Spartans, and now everyone is talking about how easily Athens can conquer Sicily. Homer was right; men tire of wine and dancing before they tire of war.

Dareia hates the idea of renewed war and the uncertainty it brings. Ari will be away again. He might get killed. Indeed,

Lysistrata

This play was eventually staged in 411 BC, five years after we have here imagined the first draft being written. By then, the Spartans were back at war with Athens, setting the scene for the attempted coup of Lysistrata. The story of Lysistrata is as described here – the women of Hellas go on a sex strike until their men agree to stop killing each other.

The play is considered to be Aristophanes' masterwork, and it has been frequently translated and anthologized. The problem with many modern versions of the work is that they reinterpret the author's meaning by being overtly feminist. Though Aristophanes was much more sympathetic to women than many of his peers, he used the idea of female dominance for comic effect.

The ancient Greek text is loaded with breathtakingly obscene jokes, which sensitive translators tend to gloss over. Imagine Shakespeare writing pornography with a political twist to get an idea of the original.

if the war goes very badly, Dareia and Chryseis might not live through it either.

'War's a man's affair,' Chryseis says, her back to Dareia in the lamplight.

'So we sit quietly at home, lonely and forgotten,' Chryseis says, 'expected to endure their tantrums and childish antics. Though we bite our tongues, we can easily work out how the war is going. Even at home he talks of nothing but. Unless he comes from the Assembly with some fresh tale of a decision even more stupid than the last, and one that's going to rush us to destruction all the faster. Yet if we should ask what's going to be inscribed on the treaty-stone, all we get is an irritable glare and the warning to keep to our shuttle and loom – or our buttocks will be sore and hot for hours afterwards.'

Dareia is surprised by her companion's rant. She didn't know Chryseis could be so eloquent. Then she realizes that, while she was reading her scroll, Chryseis had picked up the playwright's rough notes and was quoting from them. Looking over Chryseis' shoulder at the well-blotted script, Dareia sees that Aristophanes has scribbled 'Goes in iambs for tetrameter'. Whatever that means.

Dareia giggles. She has realized why she didn't recognize her master's words. He's not put a dirty joke in there yet. That's what Aristophanes does best; he expresses something filthy in such elegant verse that the audience don't know whether to be admiring or outraged.

She assesses her master's work with a critical eye. She's no expert critic, but life at home will be so much better if Aristophanes' new play is received well. A lot depends on the chorus. The chorus can make or break a play, depending on how well they are coached. And here's the lines of the chorus – but wait. Startled, Dareia roots through the pile on the desk. Here's another one. She realizes that Aristophanes is going for one chorus of men, and another of women. That's twice the number of choruses, so twice the possibility of something going wrong. But it's innovative, and Dareia thinks theatre-goers will give Aristophanes credit for that.

Dareia wants Aristophanes to win the Dionysia again. It's so much better than the Lenaia. At the Dionysia the leading playwrights of Athens present their work. The Lenaia is a lesser festival that happens in the month of Gamelion (roughly January), two months before the Dionysia. Often a playwright will test his personal popularity at the Lenaia before going all out at the Dionysia.

She considers her master's options and his character. He might go with this at the Lenaia. Whether this play is popular or not, it seems to be something he wants to get off his chest. But it's risky, too. If peace is maintained, this whole play won't even be worth entering. Aristophanes will have wasted his time. She says as much to Chryseis, who disagrees.

'No, you know him. He will fiddle with it for years until there's a bad war. There's always a war, even if we win Sicily without a serious fight.'

Dareia gives a mock cheer. 'Tha' Spartaaans will get to et, yawl see!'

'Oh, in the name of Hermes Psychopompus! That accent is abominable. Still, we've got a while yet. When he's been working this late, he's never up early. Want to try being Lampito again?'

THE DOCTOR TREATS
THE ARREPHOROS

'Have you noticed how it's only bad news that can't wait? Your son gets crowned as victor in the games, or wins the prize for poetry, and still people wait until the next morning before they tell you. If someone pounds on your door when the Harp is still high, then – even before you've pulled your head out of the blankets – you know it's bad news.'

Phoikos the doctor squints over the rooftops at the bluish Harp star. According to myth, the stars in its constellation make up the fabled lyre of Orpheus, the singer whose music charmed the birds from the trees. Even the gods were moved to tears when Orpheus played his harp to console himself for the untimely death of his wife.

This won't be the first, nor the last time that Phoikos has been dragged from his bed, but this is the first time he has been roused by guards from the Temple of Athena on the Acropolis. A priestess of Athena Polias (Athena of the City) has been unexpectedly taken ill, and Phoikos is dreading what he might find. The death of any priestess is a terrible event, but this particular death would be all the more devastating because the priestess is only eleven years old.

She is one of the Arrephoroi, a 'bearer of the secret things'. Depending on how you look at it, there are two or four of these mini-priestesses, aged anywhere between seven and eleven. There's the serving pair, of which Phoikos' yet unmet patient is one, and there's the training pair, who will replace them at the end of the four-year cycle.

The girls are from the most aristocratic families in Athens. Once selected to serve Athena they leave their homes to live with the goddess. Their new homes are on the Acropolis in a select area called the Erechtheion. In the ancient days, when all Athenians lived in the High City – 'high city' is what 'Acropolis' actually means – the Erechtheion was a functional little residential area. Now only city guards and the priestesses are there at night. The Persians destroyed the original buildings when they captured Athens two generations ago, so now the priestesses live in new custom-built quarters, complete with their own playground.

The Arrephorion

This building has been excavated in modern times. The priestesses lived in a small square hall with a four-column colonnade fronted by a rectangular courtyard. Because of the fragile nature of the site and the ease with which the limestone foundations are corroded by rain, it was decided in 2006 that the Arrephorion should once again be carefully buried under the earth that has preserved it for the past 2,000 years.

Phoikos wonders if it's a good idea to separate girls from their parents while they are still children. Of course, aristocratic girls leave home anyway at age fourteen to become wives in their own households, but at age seven? He thinks of his three-year-old daughter slumbering in her cot at home and shudders at the thought of parting from her while she is still so young.

That, however, is what the goddess Athena requires. The girls have to be aged seven because they need two years of training before they take up their duties. Each girl must complete her final two years of service by the age of eleven in case she is a premature developer. If a priestess starts menstruation early, she might sabotage the city's entire religious calendar, for the Arrephoroi of Athena have to be not only virgins but infertile. Prepubescent girls are the only way to guarantee a female who is both.

That's the other reason for the training pair. If a priestess is unable to serve, then her trainee steps up into her station, while the religious authorities take a deep breath and pray that nothing will go wrong while the newcomer finds her way into the job.

The doctor's little group moves along the road between the looming shadows of the Acropolis to the right and the hill of the Areopagus to the left. Where their road meets with the broad highway of the Panathenaic Way another group awaits, cloaked and shadowed in the torchlight; more watchmen, and the parents of the sick child.

Would the parents be there, wonders Phoikos, if the girl were not a sacred priestess who brings so much honour to her family? Each candidate for the job is handpicked by the *Archon Basileus*, 'the King's magistrate'. (No matter that Athens hasn't had a king for centuries. The royal magistrate is still highly influential in religious matters, murder cases and other civic functions.) Once chosen by the Archon, potential Arrephoroi are exempt from Pericles' stricture that 'a virtuous woman is never mentioned, whether in praise or condemnation'. Instead the entire Athenian Assembly discusses the merits of each girl before voting for the sacred two. An Arrephoros in the family is a very big deal.

Panarista daughter of Mantias of Marathon; her father and her mother, Theodote daughter of Dositheos [of Myrrhinoutta], and her brothers, Kleomenes and [name unclear] dedicated [this statue], when she had been arrephoros for Athena Polias.

INSCRIPTION BENEATH A STATUE COMMEMORATING THE
SERVICE OF AN ARREPHOROS, IG 2(2) 3488

On the other hand, for a family, a very sick priestess is even worse than her not being chosen in the first place, for her illness means that she has been rejected by the goddess herself. No wonder the parents are alarmed. Yet as he comes closer, Phoikos is ashamed of his cynicism. The mother's face shows shining tear tracks in the torchlight, and her husband holds her tenderly and protectively.

'What do we know?' the father asks the doctor, his voice low but urgent.

'I've yet to see her. Some delirium, the guards tell me, but nothing indicative of infection. She was incoherent when they found her, and unconscious soon afterwards. The attack was sudden, for she was playing a ballgame with her companions in the afternoon. They are tending to her now.'

'A brain fever?'

'I cannot rule that out. We need to see how fast the illness is progressing, and whether it approaches a crisis. Should that happen, we have a runner standing by. I have a guest from the island of Kos, the man called Hippocrates. If the case is severe I shall summon him for a consultation. First though, I need to make my own observations.'

PALPATING THE ABDOMEN OF A YOUNG PATIENT

'Just four months,' the mother sobs. 'In four months she would carry her basket and come home to me. She was the sweetest of little girls.' Phoikos silently notes the use of the past tense.

The basket to which the mother refers contains the 'mysterious things', the *arreta*. One mystery of the Arrephoroi is that no one in Athens speaks of their sacred ceremony, yet everyone knows what is involved. Every four years, in the dark of night the young priestesses dress in garments of purest white which they themselves have woven for this occasion. In silence they proceed to the altar of the goddess, where two covered baskets are waiting. The contents of the baskets are known only to Athena herself.

Taking the baskets, the pair proceed. They have practised their route so often that darkness is no obstacle. The baskets are heavy, but the girls balance the burden on their heads, in the manner of women carrying water from the fountains. In silence they walk towards the north slope of the Acropolis, where they vanish as if the earth has swallowed them up. Which it has. The girls have stepped into an underground passage, and are carefully making their way down the worn stone steps. The steps are worn because the passage is old – older than anyone can remember. In fact, the passage, adapted from a natural cave, has been in continuous use for around a thousand years. Perhaps the original inhabitants of the Acropolis used it to fetch water, for there is a disused well near the exit where the passage opens into the gardens of the Sanctuary of Aphrodite. According to legend, the spring that supplied water for the well dried up after an earthquake 700 years ago.

At the end of the passage two other baskets wait. Silently the girls remove the burdens from their heads. They set these down and take up these other baskets instead. Then comes the tricky journey through the dark passage back up to the altar of Athena Polias. There the new baskets are placed on the altar, and adult priests step forward to complete the ceremony. Their vital task accomplished, the Arrephoroi have completed their duties and are now discharged from their role.

The Sacred Rite

The most detailed description of this rite comes from Pausanias' *Guide to Greece* (1.27.3). The ritual and other events are as described in this chapter.

One might reasonably ask what this mysterious ritual has accomplished. To understand, we must look at the first Arrephoroi, sisters called Herse and Aglauros. In mythological times when Athens was young, the two girls were given charge of a mysterious basket by Athena herself. They were told never to look inside but to care for the basket kept near the sacred olive tree of Athena – a tree that still grows beside her shrine.

Herse and Aglauros became overwhelmed with curiosity about the basket's contents. They took the basket deep inside the underground cave, so that they could check the contents out of the sight of Athena. Whatever the pair saw in the basket drove them insane, for the girls rushed up the stairs and on attaining the heights of the Acropolis they leapt to their deaths.

It is generally assumed that the basket contained the baby Erichthonius, who later became the first king of Athens. After one of the gods had tried unsuccessfully to rape her, Athena threw down a cloth stained with her attacker's semen. So fertile was the divine sperm that a child was conceived from contact with the earth. It may be that owing to the bizarre circumstances of his birth, Erichthonius took a while to assume an acceptable shape. Until then, well, it was best that he remained concealed in a basket.

Athena was deeply annoyed by Herse and Aglauros' breach of promise. Since the gods are never very discriminating in their displays of ill temper, Athena threatened her revenge on the whole of Athens. Which is where the current Arrephoroi come in. They embody a solemn proof that the daughters of Athens can carry the sacred baskets of Athena, and never, ever peek at the contents. In return, Athena stays her wrath and allows dew to fall on the sacred olive tree. Thereafter the tree will bloom, along with all the olives of Attica.

The olive is central to Athenian life. Olives are eaten with almost every meal, and the oil used in cooking, cleaning, washing, medicine and lighting. It is desperately important that Athena bless the tree with a soaking dewfall – hence the vital role of the Arrephoroi, whose name literally means 'dew-bearers'.

Athena called on Cecrops to witness that she was taking possession of the city, and she planted that olive tree which still grows in the Pandrosion ... The land was adjudged to belong to Athena because she was the first to bestow the olive.

PSEUDO-APOLLODORUS *BIBLIOTHECA* 3.14

Of course, the girls can spend only so long rehearsing the most crucial night of their lives. They are also involved in weaving the sacred robe presented to Athena during the festival of the Chalkeia, and they prepare sacred cakes used in sacrifice. The priestesses receive the usual education of Athenian girls, and in their free time they scamper all over the Acropolis and also the Agora (although there they are heavily veiled and accompanied by serious bodyguards). Any gold jewellery the girls might buy on such visits is considered sacred.

Having proven themselves in the service of the goddess, some Arrephoroi might go on to other sacred duties. Some take a starring role at the great festival of Athena as the Kanephoros, who carries the basket symbolic of the bounty Athena has bestowed upon her people. Altogether, these little priestesses are an essential component of Athenian life, so when one falls suddenly and severely ill, it bodes calamity for the entire city. No wonder the guards wasted no time in getting Phoikos from his bed.

'Leave us for a moment,' the doctor orders as he stands at the doorway of the small bedroom, barely able to see his patient through the press of concerned people clustered around her bed.

Phoikos waits for the room to empty. Then he steps inside and gently puts an arm around the unconscious girl and cautiously sits her up. The flesh is warm beneath her shift and her face is slightly flushed. Breathing, heavy yet even. Suddenly and without the slightest warning, the unconscious girl throws up, copiously. Quickly, Phoikos turns his patient, lying her across his knee and patting her back to clear her airways. Then he looks at his vomit-sodden tunic. 'Ah,' he says, making one of the speediest diagnoses of his career.

Several minutes later Phoikos confronts the small crowd gathered outside the room. Apart from a tunic wadded up in one hand he is completely naked. This causes him no embarrassment whatsoever, as public nudity is no uncommon state for an Athenian male. He gestures with the tunic. 'She is now in no danger and should be fully recovered in a day or two. Until then I prescribe water and bed rest, with a little porridge when she can handle it. The girl has purged herself, and the crisis has passed.'

The mother gives a wail of relief, and timidly asks, 'Purged? Was it an evil spirit?'

Phoikos pauses for several seconds, then nods curtly. 'That is what I shall be reporting to the priests. There is now much to discuss.' None of which, Phoikos reflects privately, will be good for the priestess. She is in for an unpleasant few days of purification.

The doctor nods at the commander of the temple guard. 'A word, if I may?'

The two walk into the porch of the Erechtheion and stand in the shadows. The bulk of the Parthenon is on their left, and the Altar of Athena before them. 'It would be best if word of the girl's sickness did not get out,' Phoikos murmurs. 'And you need to talk to your men.'

'Of course,' replies the officer. 'You want a search of the Acropolis in case the sorcerer still lurks about?'

'Sorcerer?'

'The one who caused the possession of the girl.'

'No', says the doctor. 'I want you to find out how she got hold of *this*.' He holds up by the strap a little wine flask made of rawhide, of the type that soldiers carry.

THE COMMODORE
SETS OUT

A sleek shape breaks through the sea-mist, with another alongside, and another. Then a pause and another set of three follow, about a hundred paces behind. They are triremes, a squadron of six heading east, barely visible in the darkness as they cut across the bay of Phalerum.

They are heavily laden, these ships, and carrying sail as well as oars. This is no routine patrol, but a long-distance expedition to Thrace and the mines of Thasos.

The commodore in command of the trireme squadron squints carefully through the pre-dawn mist, watching intently the small lines of white that mark the foam of waves breaking on the shore. He is concentrating on keeping his distance from that darkened beach. At this dangerous start of the voyage he has to stay offshore and yet not so far out into the Saronic Gulf that he will fail to see the Zoster promontory. He needs an early sighting to know when to make a timely starboard turn and put the dangerous Phaura islet and its accompanying shoals on his port bow. There are good reasons why warships seldom venture out of port before daybreak, and some of those reasons are the splintered hulls decorating the rocks between the Zoster promontory and Phaura.

The commodore clings to a dew-wet rope at the cathead and squints into the darkness, quietly cursing the mist. By his count there are around two and a half hours until sunrise, and half that time before the pre-dawn light helps with navigation. By then they should be rounding craggy Cape Sounion, where the majestic Temple of Poseidon stands outlined against the sky.

The commodore looks back along the deck of his warship. Actually, 'deck' is the wrong word, for apart from small fighting platforms fore and aft, most of the trireme is open to the sky. From end to end of the open space runs a cable almost as thick as his forearm. That's the *hypozomata* and, as it should be, the cable is quietly humming with tension. This cable keeps things literally shipshape – pulling bow and stern together and helping to keep the planks of the hull tight against one another. Without the *hypozomata* the trireme would 'hog', or bend upwards in the middle, because the middle of any ship is naturally more buoyant than the thinner parts at the front and back.

On each side of the *hypozomata* the rowers work quietly in unison. Seated almost at the waterline are the *thalmian* rowers, their oars sleeved in leather to prevent waves from splashing through the oar holes into the ship. Next come the *zygian* rowers. Imagine that the *zygian* rower had been sitting in the lap of the *thalmian* rower, and someone lifted him and moved his still-crouching body up and forward three feet. That would give you the relative position of the lower two banks of rowers and an understanding of why it is considered violently anti-social for a *zygian* rower to eat beans. The top

SHALLOW RELIC SHOWING WHY *THRANITES* WERE TOP DOGS AMONG OARSMEN

oarsman is the *thranite*, who sits above and between the other two oarsmen.

Each level of rowers has oars of slightly different weight and length, designed so that all three banks, comprising 170 oars in all, dip into the water at the same time. This allows 35 metres of trireme to power through the water at a top speed of almost 15 kmh or cruise all day at around half that speed. The different techniques involved in operating each type of oar mean that rowers cannot easily change positions, much as the *thalmians* (whose name means 'hold' from the part of the ship where they are stationed) might envy the *zygians* (who get their name from the hull-supporting beams on which they sit). Both lower levels envy the 'deckers', or *thranites*, who get to enjoy sea-air at deck level, and are seated slightly outboard from their fellow rowers so that their oars are not even that much longer or heavier.

Running a trireme is expensive, because rowers are skilled professionals who expect to be well-paid for their demanding work. You can't employ slaves for the job because slaves develop the sort of bloody-minded obtuseness that leads to fouled oars, disjointed rowing and an unfortunate lack of effort at mission-critical moments.

Even with everyone trying their best it is hard to keep the rhythm, let alone speed it up or slow it down. The trireme comes with a flautist who keeps the appropriate time, but it's not always easy to hear him as the oars bang against the rowlocks, waves thump the sides of the ship, and the wind whistles across the decking. Often the rowers chant a timing song to keep their rhythm.

$\longleftrightarrow$

Dip your oar, for the most charming of songs ...
Brekekekex, ko-ax, ko-ax,
Brekekekex, ko-ax, ko-ax!

My hands are blistered and very sore
My bum below is sweltering so, I know

Soon I'll have to lift, and let it roar ...
Brekekekex, ko-ax, ko-ax.

ARISTOPHANES *THE FROGS* L.225 PASSIM

$\longleftrightarrow$

The trireme represents the peak of Athenian technology, and since this is Athenian technology, these triremes are the most advanced items of marine hardware in the world. Such weaponry does not come cheap. The commodore finds it easiest to think of trireme costs by the talent, which is 6,000 Attic drachmas, or enough to keep a skilled workman and his family for sixteen years.

A basic trireme, with a hull of wood imported cheaply from Macedonia, costs a talent. Equipping all the essentials such as sails, oars, ropes and the formidable ram upfront costs another talent. Finally, keeping the thing afloat with a full crew costs around another talent – every month. The Athenian state pays the basic wage of the rowers, but many trierarchs, the ships' captains, pay a bonus for a superior crew.

Building a trireme (a well-built ship can last a quarter-century or so) is generally the job of the wealthiest citizens of Athens. Usually the city council 'suggest' to picked millionaires that they might like to earn the approval of the voters by sponsoring another trireme to add to the 220 ships that Athens already has on the water.

In return for building the ship the sponsor gets to name it, and he commands it when built. This trireme is the *Philhippa*, the Lady of Horses, as a wealthy horse-breeder commissioned it. Since the horse-breeder is elderly and frail, the trierarch is the breeder's idiot son. One reason that the commodore has chosen to command his little squadron of ships from the *Philhippa* is to stop the captain from doing anything egregiously stupid.

Successful Athenians generally have no objection to sponsoring a trireme. Among the Athenian elite, competition for prestige is ferocious, and means for competing are few. So not only do they kit out triremes, but each millionaire makes his trireme into a floating advertisement for his power and general excellence. As the commodore's own uncle Thucydides, who was also an admiral, has remarked, 'Everyone spends a fortune on his own trireme, on its emblems and rigging, each wanting their own to look better and move faster than the rest.'[3]

Triremes hold the Athenian empire together. Everyone knows of the *Paralus* and the *Salaminia* – two triremes famous for their speed. As well as participating in religious festivals, the speedy pair are constantly on the move, carrying messages and diplomats around the island cities of the Aegean Sea. (Though, sacred or not, when it comes to battle the *Salaminia* and *Paralus* take their places in the fighting line along with the rest of the fleet.)

Some Athenian Trireme Names

(Athenian ships were usually feminine)

Lycania: the She-wolf

Aura: the Breeze

Amphitrite: named after the wife of Poseidon the sea god.

Meitta: the Bee

Achilleia: the feminine of the warrior Achilles

Salaminia: the Samaminian – Salamis was the location of a famous Athenian naval victory

Elutheria: Freedom

Niceso: I shall win

TABULAE CURATORUM NAVALIUM IG2 1614–1628 PASSIM

The other ships of the Athenian fleet ferry troops to far-flung locations and keep a wary eye on Persian warships moored at Tyre and other stations on the Levant. They ferry diplomats to explain to protesting Athenian allies (also known as 'subjects') why their contributions (also known as 'tribute') have gone up yet again. In such discussions, the triremes lurk offshore as a practical argument that while paying the tribute is painful, not paying will be much, much worse.

Thasos, where the present naval squadron is bound, is a good example. Thasos lies off the Thracian coast east of Macedonia, and the island is prosperous. It abounds in timber and has rich goldmines. After the Persian wars, Thasos was invited to become a member of the anti-Persian League led by Athens. Wanting protection from Persia, the Thasians happily agreed until they found that the Athenians had unilaterally decided that Thasian markets and mines on the nearby mainland now belonged to Athens.

That was when the people of Thasos found that withdrawing from the League (also known as 'the Athenian empire') was not an option. When they tried to withdraw anyway, the Athenian triremes arrived. After a two-year siege the Thasians had their city walls demolished, their navy confiscated and an annual tax of thirty silver talents imposed. Thasos is once again a member in good standing with the League, and compared with some other recalcitrant members, the Thasians feel they got off lightly.

The commodore will drop off supplies for the small Athenian garrison in the citadel at the island's harbour, which helps to maintain Thasian enthusiasm for League membership. The squadron will sweep around the harbour to remind the islanders of the watchful eye of Athens, and then proceed along the coast of Thrace. Lycian pirate barques have been preying on shipping. As well as interrogating local fishermen for information, the men of the squadron will check every obscure bay along the coast in the hope of finding the pirate hideout.

Because he expected to fight he left his large sails behind in Athens [triremes did not carry sail in battle as it just slowed the rowers down]. He also barely made use of the smaller sails, even in a good wind. By doing the voyage on oar-power he both toned up his men and did the trip faster. For dinner and lunch he would … order the ships to … race for the shore. The victors had the considerable prize of being the first to draw water and the first to get their meal …

If the weather was good and there was a favourable breeze, he would set out again right after dinner, resting the rowers in shifts. In the day he would signal the fleet to form column or line of battle, so that even as they approached enemy waters they had become skilled at fleet manoeuvres.

THE ATHENIAN ADMIRAL IPHICRATES TRAINS HIS FLEET,
XENOPHON *HELLENICA* 6.2.26 FF

Triremes are good for this work, because they are light and strong. Even fully loaded, a trireme can float in little more than four cubits of water (a cubit is the distance from the middle finger to the elbow of a normal-sized man), which means that a trireme can venture into very shallow bays and if it does get stuck on a sandbank, everyone gets off. If that is itself not enough to re-float the ship, the crew simply pick it up and carry it to deeper water.

Another advantage of the all-wood trireme is that it is buoyancy-positive. That is, a trireme does not rely on displacing more than its weight of water to remain afloat. If an enemy ram puts a huge hole in the bottom of the hull, a trireme still won't sink, even if the waterlogged hulk is no longer particularly seaworthy.[4]

The commodore has some reservations about a part of the expedition that he has not mentioned to the Athenian authorities. It's nothing illegal, but perhaps something that it's better to apologize for later (if discovered) than to seek approval for in advance. Stashed under the fighting-bow is a series of little packets wrapped in oilskin cloth. They are reports from the interviews that the commodore has conducted for his uncle Thucydides.

Thucydides was commodore of a fleet operating along the Thracian coast during the recent war. Sadly, Thucydides had an abundance of natural caution and a meticulous approach to warfare. Consequently, he was too late to relieve a city that a more impulsive commander might have prevented from falling into Spartan hands. An unsympathetic Athenian Assembly responded by ordering Thucydides into exile.

Ever since, Thucydides has been resident on his family estates in Thrace. He's hardly in isolation because all Athenians of any distinction pop in to visit him if they are in the area. It is well known that Thucydides is using his enforced idleness to write what will be the definitive history of the recent war with Sparta. Almost everyone over the age of twenty-five fought in that war, and many of these veterans visit Thucydides in case the historian needs clarification about their personal (and heroic) contribution to the conflict.

Where the historian needs further details, he asks not only Athenians and Thracians, but also Thebans, Spartans and Corinthians, who fought on the other side. The result is intended to be a balanced and unbiased account of the war. This does not greatly please the Athenian authorities who prefer to shape the narrative into one of courageous Athens standing up to the Spartan bully. That's why the commodore is a bit reticent to disclose that he is carrying his father's account of an incident eight years ago when the Thebans resoundingly defeated the Athenians in battle and the subsequent siege at Delium. The Athenians would much prefer that everyone forgot about that debacle.

Thucydides

Born the generation after Herodotus, Thucydides took a radically different approach to his predecessor. Where Herodotus was fond of anecdotes and hearsay, Thucydides considered that history should be facts examined and reported as impartially as possible. So epic was his achievement that even today some historians often treat Herodotus as a 'historical source' and Thucydides as if he were a colleague who has stepped out of the room for a moment.

What we know of Thucydides, he tells us himself – and he does not tell us much. He was of an aristocratic family; he caught the plague in 430 BC but, unlike many Athenians, he survived. He commanded a fleet against the Spartans, and was exiled for inadequate performance (Thucydides, 4.104ff). In 416, it is now between wars, but when war with Sparta resumes, Thucydides will collect details from both sides as a neutral party. He returned to Athens after the war and died suddenly around 404 with important parts of his *History* still unfinished.

The commodore also knows that Thucydides will press him for details of the ships and men being prepared for the Syracusan expedition. He will mutter 'That's classified' to each question while his uncle regards him with a predatory and unblinking gaze, looking like nothing so much as an offended hawk. The commodore sighs, knowing he is going to tell much more than he should, and yet much less than Thucydides wants. If only he had just the tides, currents and things like that accursed Zoster promontory to worry about.

THE SLAVE MINER STARTS WORK

As the commodore's squadron rounds Cape Sounion, just inland at Laurion the miners whose efforts help to pay for the triremes are starting work. Deimokos groans as he rolls off his cot. He knows that there's something wrong with him – there has been since the overseer kicked him hard just below the ribs two days ago. Deimokos knows better than to complain, although he has been urinating copious amounts of blood. Truth be told, Deimokos wants to die.

He has been a slave for ten years now, six in the mines, and has lost hope of ever leaving except as a corpse. Twelve years ago, he was a prosperous merchant with a large house, a wife and three daughters. He had slaves of his own, and he occasionally winces when he remembers the cruelties that he unthinkingly inflicted on them. Deimokos lived on Mytilene, principal city of the island of Lesbos.

Mytilene was one of the foremost cities of the anti-Persian League. It was also one of the few cities that saw through the deception by which Athens converted the League against the Persians into an empire under Athenian rule. At first, everyone welcomed Athenian leadership. These were the energetic Athenians who had fought off the Persians at Marathon, and later, even after the Persians had devastated their city, the Athenians had led the effort that decisively defeated the Persian fleet at Salamis.

One problem for small cities fighting the Persians was that the manpower used to crew the ships and form the hoplite battleline was the same manpower needed to plough the fields and fish the waters back home. To them, Athens made a disingenuous offer: 'Keep your men working in the fields. We, the Athenians, have men and ships enough to do the fighting. All you need to do is pay every year for the men and the ships that you would otherwise supply. You can meet your treaty obligations with one easy payment.'

This seemed reasonable enough, and most cities paid. But not Mytilene. That city had suffered too much in the Persian wars to willingly give up its ships and hoplites. So the people of Mytilene watched as the Athenians used the ships and men paid for by the island city-states to enforce their mastery of those same city-states. Although the Athenians had barely exchanged a blow with the Persians for the past decade, the cost of League membership kept going up, while Athens built monuments such as the Parthenon with the money.

When Athens and Sparta had gone to war, Mytilene took the opportunity to break out of the League. To his eternal regret Deimokos was one of the city councillors who believed Spartan promises of immediate support and assistance. He voted for Mytilene unilaterally to leave the League, and then waited for the promised Spartan assistance.

Naturally the Athenians were the first to arrive, and promptly laid siege to the city with that demonic energy for which their city was infamous. The Spartans never came at all. After due consideration they had decided that supporting Mytilene was too risky, so they abandoned the city to its fate. After the Athenians, Deimokos hates the Spartans most of all.

At first, the Athenians were going to kill everyone in Mytilene once they had captured it. On reflection they reconsidered, and only killed the ringleaders of the 'rebellion'. Secondary leaders such as Deimokos were enslaved. Taken to Athens, Deimokos was put to work in an apple orchard. He worked hard, hoping to gain the attention of his owner, who might promote him to household duties and perhaps eventually free him. Instead, the owner leased him to the mines.

Treat the people of Mytilene as they deserve, and as is expedient. Deciding to do otherwise is not a favour to them but a judgement upon yourselves. If they are right to rebel against you, you must be wrong to rule them. But right or wrong, if you want an empire then you have to act like it. Punish the Mytilenians. Either do as you must, or give up your empire and take up social work …

Set a compelling example that will teach your other allies that the price of rebellion is death. Once they understand this, you won't have to take time off from fighting your enemies in order to fight your friends.

THUCYDIDES *HISTORY OF THE PELOPONNESIAN WAR* 3.37

It's good money, leasing slaves. Deimokos is – was – worth 200 drachmas (every slave knows his price). Renting out Deimokos gets his owner a drachma a week. As a former merchant Deimokos knows that as an investment over the years he has returned 30 per cent plus capital to his owner. If he dies – and there's a kind of swollen stiffness in his side that suggests he will – then the mine's owners will have to pay for a replacement to compensate for their overseer's carelessness.

The land at Laurion is owned by the state, but the individual silver mines that dot the landscape in their dozens are owned by private individuals or companies. They pay the Athenian treasury for the right to extract silver on two-, three- or seven-year leases. Mines can be tiny two-man operations, or large affairs employing dozens of slaves.

Each of the ten tribes elects a vendor. These sell public contracts, and the leases for the mines and the taxes … They ratify the sale of [the right to operate] mines and workings for three years and the sale of concessions.

ARISTOTLE *ATHENIAN CONSTITUTION* 47.2

Deimokos is part of a ten-man crew. He and his fellow workers stumble down the foul-smelling tunnel (workers are not given toilet breaks) until they reach the rock face. The main shaft has split into separate tunnels, and the slaves divide into teams of two. One member of each pair will spend the next hour with a pick hewing at the solid rock. The other will scrabble behind him gathering the rock fragments in a sack. After a brief break, they will change round, and later change again until the end of their fifteen-hour day.

When an ore sack is full, the miner takes it to a cart in the central tunnel. The overseer stands by the cart, and if any pair works too slowly, he proceeds down their tunnel and administers an incentive. He also times how long it takes the cart to get to the ore-processor and back. It was because he tarried at this job that Deimokos received his beating.

The ore-processor is owned by a collective of mine-owners. Women and children sit with hammers crushing the rock into pebbles. The pebbles are poured into a trough over which flows a carefully regulated stream of water. Lighter pebbles are swept away in the current. The galena – the lead ore – and silver-bearing rock remains at the bottom, weighed down by its heavier metal content. This rock is removed for later smelting. There are only three large smelters at Laurion, and they operate all day and all night, sending Athens a never-ending stream of silver to feed the city's imperial ambitions.

Thoutimides of Sounoin has registered at Thalinos the working mine [called] 'Artemesiskon in Nape', on the stele of Eubolos, in the property of ___ [name obscured]. The boundaries are: North, the Artemisiakon mine of ___. South, the ditch between Nape and the workshop of Epicrates. East, Teleson's house and grounds. West, the workshop leased by Thoutimides of Sounoin son of Phanias.

Price: 150 drachmas.

A MINE LEASE AT LAURION. TRANSLATION FOLLOWING *CIG* II (2)
AND M. CROSBY *HESPERIA* 19, 1950

When last at the ore-processor, Deimokos had recognized a Dorian woman from the island of Melos. In his previous life as a merchant, he had visited the island to arrange a shipment of obsidian for a customer in Egypt. The woman had been the wife of the obsidian dealer. Now she was a slave.

She told Deimokos that the Athenians had come to Melos with their ships and their hoplites. They demanded the island's incorporation into the League, and a massive tribute payable immediately. Asked by what right they made this demand of fellow Greeks, the Athenians contemptuously replied:

We shall not trouble you with specious pretences – either of how we have a right to our empire because we overthrew the Persians, or to claim that we are now attacking you because of wrong that you have done us. We won't make a long speech which would not be believed; and in return we hope that you won't think to influence us by saying ... that you have done us no wrong.

You know as well as we do how the world goes. Justice is only in question between equals in power. Otherwise the strong do what they can and the weak suffer what they must.[5]

In response to this arrogance, the Melians had literally chosen liberty or death. They fought as free men until their inevitable defeat. Thereafter the Athenians slaughtered the surviving men and brought the women and children to the slave pits in Laurion. It was imperialism at its most brutal, and it left Deimokos wondering anew what had become of his wife and daughters.

Deimokos' conversation with the Melian woman had taken longer than he had allowed for, and the overseer was fuming by the time Deimokos trundled the cart back for its next load. Preoccupied by thoughts of his lost family, Deimokos gave a casual and derogatory answer to the overseer's angry query. That caused the beating that followed.

If it cost Deimokos his life, at least it would also cost the overseer his job. An overseer has to make the slaves as productive as possible. After the cost of the lease itself, slaves make up almost all the mine's capital investment. An overseer who wantonly destroys mine equipment – and mine equipment is what Deimokos is – deserves to lose his job.

As a merchant, Deimokos often handled Athenian coin. Indeed, he often insisted on payment in 'owls', as the coins are known everywhere in the eastern Mediterranean. Stamped with the image of the owl of Athena, Athenian coins are renowned for their pure silver content and standard high quality. The usual coin is a tetradrachm – about as much as Deimokos earns for his owner in a month.

Men who travel far on trading missions talk of finding Athenian coins used in the plains of India and the ports of Arabia. When

ATHENS PRODUCED THE FINEST
SILVER IN THE KNOWN WORLD

Deimokos had handled the coins he sometimes thought of those distant, exotic places where the tetradrachms might end up. Now, when he thinks of the coins at all, he thinks of where they started out – at the end of a dank tunnel where a naked man toils with a pickaxe by the light of a single oil lamp, patiently chipping at the unyielding stone, hour after hour, day after day, on through the unending years.

Deimokos knows less of his fellow slaves than one might expect. Though they are constantly in each other's company the overseer brutally punishes conversation during working hours. At night, each man staggers to his cot exhausted after a brutally long shift. It's not a time for socializing but for sleep and gathering strength, because tomorrow it all starts again.

Five men Deimokos couldn't understand anyway – three are Thracians, as shown by the swirling tattoos on their chests and necks; another two are Lacedaemonians, slaves captured from Sparta by Athenian raids on the Peloponnese. These sometimes mutter among themselves in their incomprehensible native dialects. Another, a Boeotian, was once a shepherd. Three gangly teens, recently purchased, are native-born Athenian slaves, probably the offspring of slave agricultural workers. As a merchant Deimokos often saw slave workers rutting unashamed like beasts in the field.

Today he is partnered with the Boeotian. The shepherd knows of Deimokos' injury, and silently indicates that Deimokos should take the sack rather than the pick. With the sound of the pick clanging in his ears, Deimokos gathers the rock fragments and lets his mind wander.

Laurion. An accursed place, because here the seed sprouted that became the Athenian monster. A century ago Athens was just another mid-range Hellenic city, ranking below Thebes, Corinth or Argos. Certainly Athens was not comparable with the power of Sparta, the city that dominated most of the Peloponnese.

The silver mines were always there, but nothing special. People had been mining at Laurion for thousands of years.

Then, just before the Persian wars, a new and much richer vein of almost pure silver was discovered. Themistocles, the wily Athenian leader at the time, proposed that instead of distributing this unexpected bounty among the citizenry, the Athenian people should invest the money. Specifically, they invested the money in 200 triremes. These were meant to earn their way through raids on the Persian-dominated coast of Asia Minor and by enforcing Athenian ambitions on the timber-rich coast of Macedonia.

As it turned out, the triremes were essential in defending Athens from Persian invasion and conquest. Once Athenian sea-power had forced back the Persians, Athens was catapulted to the leadership of Greece. This rise to prominence was regarded with jealousy and suspicion by the Spartans, who saw themselves as the foremost power in Greece. In the end, it was Spartan fear of the rising power of Athens that had led to the recent war.

Yet Sparta had failed to contain the Athenians. Even as the Spartans devastated the fields of Attica, Laurion kept producing silver to pay the rowers of the triremes that protected the ships that brought grain from the Crimea, and carried the region's livestock to safety on the nearby island of Euboea. As long as Athens had her walls and her fleet, the Spartans could do no serious harm, and the mines at Laurion helped to pay for that fleet. Now the Athenians are expanding their power, devastating defenceless islands such as Melos. Where will it end?

Deimokos hoists his sack on his shoulder and gasps at the stabbing pain in his side. In a microcosm he embodies the problem faced by the subjects of the Athenian empire. Athens could never have conquered Mytilene without the silver mined at Laurion. Now Deimokos the Mytilenian mines the silver that pays for the oppression of his people, just as the people of the Aegean city-states pay the tribute that allows Athens to afford the military power that ensures that the tribute keeps coming.

Deimokos knows little of the architectural wonders rising on the Acropolis and cares nothing for the advances in sculpture, philosophy and mathematics that are driving the human race forward at an unprecedented pace. As he stumbles down the shadowy tunnel, stooped under the weight of his ore sack, Deimokos knows only how these things have been paid for.

THE VASE PAINTER
BEGINS A PROJECT

He calls himself 'the third Polygnotus'. If you wield a paintbrush in Athens, you cannot claim that name without being extraordinarily good at what you do. The name has resonance. The first Polygnotus was from Thasos. He didn't do vases, which he probably considered beneath him. But then, that Polygnotus was exceptionally good at murals.

Walk along the Panhellenic Way towards the Parthenon and as you enter the Agora, between the Royal Stoa and the Stoa of Hermes, the Painted Stoa is in front of you and slightly to the left. A stoa is a long, roofed colonnade, which allows public business to be conducted even in foul weather. These stoas are decorated, and none more so than the Painted Stoa. It is famous throughout the Greek world for its epic paintings by that famed artistic duo, Micon of Athens and Polygnotus of Thasos.

The first Polygnotus contribution was an epic work depicting the fall of Troy. The artist also contributed to a depiction of the Battle of Marathon by Panaeus, a close relative of that Pheidias who made the statue of Athena Parthenos and the Zeus at Olympia. In fact, Panaeus also painted much of the Olympia statue. Polygnotus did not paint on commission, as he was independently wealthy and did not need the money. Rather, he painted to exercise his prodigious talent, and to give back to the city that adopted him.

The second Polygnotus was a specialist in large vases: amphorae, hydria – the pots used for hauling water – and kraters, the large open bowls used for mixing wine at parties.[6] Smaller vessels are for drinking, or making sacred libations to the gods.

Polygnotus the second was a busy man because pottery is ubiquitous in Athenian life. The very rich like their bowls made of expensive metals, but everyone else uses pottery. Pots are everywhere, from decorative urns designed to awe guests in the *andron* to lumpy cookery pots and the (sometimes remarkably elegant) chamber pots beneath the beds. In fact, the 'third Polygnotus' has seen a pottery drinking cup that depicts a woman using a chamber pot. The range of subjects on Athenian crockery is remarkably diverse.

Rather like Attic silver, Athenian pottery is coveted across the Mediterranean world for its quality – not of the clay but the artwork upon it. Thousands of vases leave Athens every year, destined for places as far apart as Iberia and India.

To balance his workload, Polygnotus the second spent less time painting vases and more time roaming his workshop, dealing backhanded slaps and offhand praise to a dozen young painters whom he was training in his style. His best student was a youth called Kleophon. Later Kleophon launched his own studio in a building not far from the 'factory' of his master. (So many potters and painters work hereabouts that the area is commonly called the 'Keremeikos', the potters' district.) Since the death of his former tutor four years ago, Kleophon has taken to calling himself 'the third Polygnotus'.

Today Kleophon is in early. He has a long day ahead. Like his late master, Kleophon works mainly with large vases, in this case a decorative krater of the type known as a 'volute' (from the tight-curled handles at the top that resemble volutes, the curls at the top of architectural columns). The client is the playwright Euripides, who wants a vase to celebrate his new play *Herakles*. When Kleophon suggested painting something related to the Herakles myth, the elderly playwright disagreed. Having worked with the over-muscled hero for the past year, Euripides wanted something different for a change.

In the end, the pair agreed on a painting showing a procession to Apollo, god of theatre and the arts. The god will be seated in a peristyle that contains two bronze tripods of the kind awarded to winning playwrights at the Dionysia. The overall painting is complex, so Kleophon needs an early start.

Naturally, he will not paint the figures themselves, but the space around them. Like all contemporary vase painters, he uses the red-figure style. This involves painting on a deep, lustrous slip. This 'slip' is not the consequence of incautiously treading on the contents of an unsocially emptied chamber pot (a sadly common experience), but a special clay – a highly refined slurry painted over the normal clay of the vase that turns black in the intense heat of a furnace.

The actual process is more complex. Left to itself the slip bakes very much as does normal clay. To get that deep black, the furnace is first left open, allowing the clay to bake red. It bakes red because Athenian clay is secondary clay, washed downriver during heavy rains. The clay picks up iron particles in the process because the river also washes over beds of iron ore. When baked these iron fragments oxidize and give the clay its distinctive rusty colour. Compare this with, for example, Corinthian pots of clay dug from the original beds. Rich in kaolin and containing little iron, Corinthian pots are creamy white.

KLEOPHON'S COMPLETED PROJECT, 2,500 YEARS LATER

The slip used to paint a red-figure vase is finer than the clay of the rest of the vase, and bakes faster. When the furnace is closed, the air supply is limited and uncured 'green' wood is added to the fire. Now the slip develops its shiny black texture through the chemical process of reduction. Once the slip has changed colour, the fire is reopened and baking is completed at a lower temperature.

In the dawn light, Kleophon circles his pot like a predator assessing angles of attack. The unbaked clay was prepared by his potter the previous evening. Over the past few days he has been refining river-clay by mixing it with water and removing impurities as they sink to the bottom of the mixing bowl. For crude cooking pots, this is done once – if at all. This is a prestige project, however, that will advertise the good taste of Euripides and the skill of Kleophon. The silky-smooth clay has been purified half a dozen times.

Once he adjudged the clay to be sufficiently fine, the potter laid it on a flat wheel some two feet wide. An apprentice turned the wheel at a careful and constant speed while the potter drew up the clay with his hands. After the completed bowl had been drying for ten hours and had a firm, leathery texture, the potter took a fine chamois leather cloth and 'burnished' the clay. This lines up the microscopic platelets on the surface, making it harder and smoother. The base and handles lie nearby on cloth cushioned by sand, waiting to be affixed once they will not get in the painter's way.

Kleophon studies a set of six clay tiles showing the two pictures that he intends to transfer on to the clay. On the main, upper panel, Apollo himself is to recline in the peristyle (technically known as a *sacrellum*), which is shaped like one of the little temples in his honour called Odeons.

The pictures show that the procession is formed of six

unbearded adolescents garlanded with wreaths and wearing thin, ceremonial tunics that leave one shoulder bare but reach to the ankles. At the head of the procession is a woman carrying a sacrificial basket on her head. Kleophon frowns at the woman. Her multilayered, pleated dress with rich embroidery is going to take hours of painstaking work to transfer to the vase – and mistakes on clay are demonically hard to hide.

A figure welcoming the procession on behalf of Apollo stands beside the bronze tripods. Kleophon wants this to suggest Euripides, but not resemble him so closely that the vase becomes a vanity portrait. So the man is older than the youths in the procession, but not so old as Euripides. The beard is black instead of grey (anyway, grey needs a specially coloured clay slip and Kleophon is busy enough this morning). The man's walking staff is a type that Euripides favours, shoulder height with a T-shaped crossbar at the top.

Apollo himself (and Kleophon offers a mental apology to the god for this) is handsome but nondescript. In subtle ways the vase will draw attention away from the god and towards the non-portrait of the sponsor who commissioned the work. So the woman bearing the basket looks at 'Euripides', as does Apollo himself. Having everyone stare at the central figure would be a bit obvious, so Kleophon has the first man in the procession look not at Euripides or Apollo, but back over his shoulder. Meanwhile the branch of sacred laurel which Apollo holds inclines away from himself towards Euripides.

Overhead, Apollo has slung the quiver of his bow on the rafters of the peristyle so that the bow also points away from the god and towards Euripides. Between Apollo and the playwright is the Omphalos stone, the traditional marker of the 'navel of the world' at Apollo's shrine in Delphi. From the stone, the eye is drawn to the person whose leg is partly obscured by it – Euripides again.

A smaller, lower panel will again suggest the Dionysia without anything so vulgar as actually depicting it. Instead, a Dionysian cortège has satyrs and prancing maenads. The maenads (female worshippers of Dionysus) are known to rend their clothes in their religious frenzy but, so as not to draw attention from the main panel, Kleophon's ladies show little more than a well-turned calf. Studying his preliminary pictures, Kleophon frowns, and with a charcoal stick adjusts the angle of the staff carried by one of the dancers so that – like the upturned palms of the dancers – it points to 'Euripides' in the panel above.

O Attic shape! Fair attitude! with brede
Of marble men and maidens overwrought,
With forest branches and the trodden weed;
Thou, silent form, dost tease us out of thought
As doth eternity: Cold Pastoral!
When old age shall this generation waste,
Thou shalt remain, in midst of other woe
Than ours, a friend to man, to whom thou say'st,
'Beauty is truth, truth beauty – that is all
Ye know on earth, and all ye need to know.'

JOHN KEATS 'ODE ON A GRECIAN URN' 1819

Looking at the vase, Kleophon projects a mental image of the painting on to its surface, through long practice mentally adjusting for the curvature of the vase. He pauses, and with a muttered curse bends to study the vase's surface. Where one patch of the vase surface was a bit too dry, the potter had moistened his leather strip to correct it. In the process, he allowed a drop of water to fall on to the unbaked clay. The drop instantly soaked into the dry surface. It created a blemish, but the potter was too experienced to try to correct it. He knew that Kleophon would pick up the mark and arrange his black slip to cover it, so rather than disfigure the surface further, the potter had simply turned the vase so that the stain would be clearly visible in the morning light from the window.

Now the fun begins. Kleophon picks up a charcoal stick and delicately marks the rough outlines of his picture on to the clay. Later he will dip into the slurry a 'brush' made with a single hair from a horse's tail and draw his pictures with flowing freehand strokes. Occasionally, where a line is particularly important, Kleophon will score it into the clay with a fine needle. (He will fill in the groove with slip later, so that the surface is uniformly smooth.)

Kleophon is proud of his flowing, natural style. This is a lot easier to achieve on red-figure vases. The black figures of previous generations were stiffer and literally archaic in style, because all red lines on the black figures had to be painstakingly scratched out from the black slip once it had partly dried. It is so much easier just to paint the black around the figures and insert single lines within.

When red figures were introduced three generations ago by pioneers such as Euphronios, it produced controversy in the tight world of pottery. Yet the naturalistic poses and very human emotions which Kleophon is able to put on to the figures on his vases would be impossible otherwise. Kleophon knows that his painting is slightly derivative, for he consciously imitates the natural yet elegant lines of the Pheidias sculptures on the Parthenon. And why not? These portraits embody the spirit of the age, a reaching towards perfection which, while unattainable, challenges the next generation to get even closer.

Kleophon steps back to look at his preliminary outlines. Maybe the future will think his efforts crude and primitive, rather as his contemporaries look down on the roughly patterned pots of earlier times. Yet Kleophon knows that his generation is setting the bar high. In his mind's eye, he can see his finished work. This vase will be a good one, he feels. Lively yet serene, the colours rich yet subtle.

Beat that, posterity!

THE SORCERESS
CASTS A SPELL

E astwards from the potters' district, Celeus strides along the road that runs alongside the Themistoclean wall. He is entering Scambonidae, a residential area tight-packed with rather dingy houses. Celeus keeps to the wall side of the street to avoid having to leap aside every time someone knocks on a door and it opens outwards.

Athenian street doors usually open to a small courtyard around which the house is built. Even poor families stick to this pattern, although several families may share a single house. The street door is the only access to the premises and, in a largely unpoliced city, this door is as secure as possible. It is not unknown, however, for gangs of thugs to break down a door and loot the premises.

A door that opens into the street is harder to break down than one opening inwards into the courtyard. Consequently, most Athenians opt for safety rather than the convenience of pedestrians on the road outside. It is advisable to knock loudly on the door before leaving a house, since pedestrians tend to take violent umbrage to a door being opened in their faces without warning.

At present, doors are opening rapidly as laggards rush to begin the day. Most people started work an hour ago, since Athenians believe in rising before the sun. As a tavern owner, Celeus is excused neighbourly disapprobation for rising late. No one expects him on the premises for another two hours, when he will kick his surly slaves into preparing lunch.

The tavern of Celeus is not successful. Ask the patrons, and that diminishing tribe will mention cheap, bitter wine and stale bread served by slovenly staff in unhygienic surroundings. Ask Celeus himself, and he will tell you that other tavern owners are conspiring to put him out of business. While his wife was with him, the tavern was a lively, pleasant place – largely because the wife put in a sixteen-hour day while Celeus concentrated on extensively sampling the tavern's wine.

Now, Celeus is certain that other tavern owners envied his prosperity. They persuaded his wife to quietly decamp one summer night, taking all her savings in a small canvas bag. She now runs a relative's business supplying ships' goods in Chalcedon and she is doing rather well. Meanwhile, for Celeus, things have been going downhill.

Today he intends to strike back. He will show his enemies that they cannot sabotage his life with impunity. The address he is seeking took some work to discover. A discreetly offered silver coin persuaded one of his tavern's shadier patrons to admit that he might know someone who might know someone who might be able to help.

A few nights later, one of his slaves brought him a message – sender unknown. 'The district of Scambonidae, the street beyond the tomb of Eumolpus. Find the carpenter's workshop, and go up the stairs at the back. Be there the hour after sunrise.'

Eumolpus was an obscure hero from mythical times, and his 'tomb' is a battered and empty sarcophagus at a crossroads. As Celeus approaches, a local dog finishes urinating against the thing and lopes away. The carpenter's shop is easy to locate, for the carpenter is loudly hammering together a set of benches. As Celeus approaches, the carpenter sums him up with a hostile stare. Then he jerks his head at a set of stairs going up the back wall. With considerable trepidation, the tavernkeeper follows the silent instruction.

The room at the top is shuttered. Herbs have recently been burned, leaving a spicy, heady smell. So dark is the room that it takes Celeus a moment to notice that it is occupied. A shadowy form sits at the table, so heavily veiled that all he can see is a dark mound of cloth. Yet the voice is pleasant and surprisingly educated.

'Celeus the tavernkeeper. May the goddess Cybele bless you and yours.'

'You are the sorceress?'

A pointed silence informs the tavern owner that this was the wrong question.

Eventually the woman replies, her voice patient and level. 'Of course I am not a sorceress. A sorceress would be open to charges of impiety against the gods. The drugs that I might supply would be assumed to be poisons. I would be accused of corrupting young men and suborning slaves. And you, Celeus, would be in trouble simply for visiting me. The authorities would accuse us of performing depraved sexual acts to enable our magical activities.

'I am a mantis. All that I do is help you understand the will of the gods. Perhaps, under some circumstances, I may suggest actions that might … further the will of the gods. If you have trouble with these actions I may assist you. Is that clear?'

The veiled figure sits silently, watching her confused client grapple with what she has said. To Celeus, the (non-) sorceress seems a mysterious and threatening figure whom he has clumsily angered. She may, at this moment, be preparing a silent curse that will blight his miserable life yet further. He now regrets that he came.

HEKATE, THE TRIPLE GODDESS OF THE CROSSROADS

In actuality, the sorceress is deciding to cut down on the mixture of black henbane seeds and blue lotus flowers. When burned, the concoction makes those who inhale its smoke relaxed, uninhibited and talkative. Regrettably, in the wrong concentration or when the wrong person breathes it, the mixture is fatal. The sorceress is starting to worry about Celeus.

She asks, 'What do you want the powers of the underworld to do for you? Is there a woman you desire? A woman who will not look at you, or even acknowledge that you exist? Do you want to summon a demon who will pierce her, through the eyes, through the ears, through the stomach, breasts and womanly parts so that she thinks of you and only you? Do you want her to come to you, mad with lust, forgetting husband or other lover, to be yours and yours alone?'

Torment the spirit and the heart of Karosa, child of Thelo, until she leaps up and comes, quickly, quickly to Apalos, son of Theonilla, now, now, filled with lust and love …

Let her forget her husband, her child, but let her come melting with passion, for love and sex, especially sex with Apalos, child of Theonilla, now, now, quickly, quickly.

A 'LOVE' SPELL FROM THE FIFTH CENTURY BC,
PAPYRI GRAECAE MAGICAE 19A 50-54

The sorceress stops abruptly, realizing that she has inadvertently launched into the lines of a spell and is about to utter the mystic word *Ablanathanalba*, which compels the demon Abraxas to do just as she has described.

Celeus considers the sorceress' offer. 'Is it more expensive if the woman is now living in another city?' Then, rather regretfully, he shakes his head. 'No. I seek justice. My enemies cursed me, and I want to curse them back. Can you do that?'

'I? Of course not. Do you think I am Medea? I didn't say I can't help you, but I am a mortal, and my curses have no more power than yours. We need to call upon the right supernatural entities, present your case, and let them smite your enemies. Some of these entities can smite rather inventively.'

Celeus regards her warily. 'Which ... entities did you have in mind?'

'Hekate, Mormo and Hermes,' replies the sorceress promptly. She is already running through a mental inventory of what she will need. Most of it is in the cupboard behind her.

'Mormo,' says Celeus thoughtfully. 'My mother used to frighten me with her when I was a child. If I was naughty, or teased my sister, she would tell me that Mormo would come in the night and bite off my nose. I'd get sick with fear.'

'I need to prepare for the conjuration,' says the sorceress. 'Go downstairs and tell the carpenter to fetch a black hen from the coop across the courtyard. And leave one of those silver drachmas you promised on the table. I'll not have you wasting my time should you decide not to come back.'

Actually, Mormo is quite unnecessary for this curse. Really it will need Hekate, the witch-goddess and patroness of sorceresses, and Hermes, both in his role as god of trade and business and as Hermes Psychopompus, the guide of souls. But the sorceress has recently learned an invocation to Mormo. The ceremony is brief yet impressive, and she wants to try it out.

Spirit of the streets, the shining one who wanders by night
Enemy of light, and friend and consort of shadows
Who revels in the howl of dogs when blood flows red
Who walks among tombs and corpses turned to dust
Who pants for blood, and freezes men with fear
Gorgon and Moon, Mormo of many shapes
Come to this, our sacrificial rite![7]

Once the hen has been decapitated, the sorceress turns towards the crude hearth at the back of the room and casts a cupful of boiling water mixed with hen's blood into the little crucible she has set over the fire. Celeus gives a smothered shriek as the blood flashes into flame and dark, evil-smelling smoke roils across the room, hanging heavy in the shadows.

'You can feel her, can you not?' rasps the sorceress. 'Mormo is here. She listens.'

The sorceress is rasping because she inadvertently inhaled some of the mixture of powdered limestone and sulphur when she added it to the crucible. Like the trembling Celeus, she is very impressed with the resultant chemical reaction. She now intends to buy lots more from her clandestine supplier. The problem is that the drugged air, the solemn sacrifice of the black hen and the sudden appearance of the dreaded Mormo in a pyrotechnic display have all combined to reduce Celeus to incoherent silence.

'Speak,' croaks the sorceress, and the terrified Celeus finds his tongue.

'Curse them! Curse the tavern owners who have cursed me. May Artemis cast her hate upon Phanagora and Demetrios especially and destroy them utterly.'

Celeus has seemingly found an outlet for his pent-up

anger and frustration, and now the words come pouring out. 'Destroy their taverns, no, destroy all their property. Lay waste to everything they own. And that smooth-talking Demetrios, bind him, bind him in such a bind. Make it strong as it can be made. Hammer that tongue silent with a *kynotos*! Yes, a *kynotos*!'

A *kynotos* is the lowest possible throw of the dice. Demetrios could talk the hide off a donkey and Celeus wants him tongue-tied, his words crude, poor and stumbling.

The sorceress stands and utters a dismissive phrase in a foreign tongue. '*Ananak Arbeoueri, Aeeioyo*. Go now lady, to your own throne and protect him, Celeus, from any harm.'[8]

Then she matter-of-factly stands, crosses the room and unbars the shutter. Both sorceress and client breathe deeply with relief as the smoky foul-smelling air disperses from the room, which in daylight looks remarkably workmanlike and mundane.

The sorceress takes a lead tablet from a drawer beneath the table and, picking up a steel stylus, begins to inscribe it carefully, glancing every now and then at her papyrus notes. Celeus observes that the hand doing the inscribing is pale and dainty, with well-manicured fingernails. He stands in silence, ignored, until the sorceress hands him the completed work.

The awed Celeus turns the little leaf of rolled lead around in his fingers. He has a curse. A genuine, first-rate curse, uttered and sanctified in the presence of Mormo, ready to be delivered to the spirits of the Underworld.

Reading the script, he is briefly baffled by a reference to 'the four-year cycle'. Then he remembers that every four years, at the festival of the Great Dionysia and the Panhellenic festival, there are great and powerful rituals that cleanse the city of malignant spirits and spells. A spell must be specifically exempted from these ritual purifications, or with the Great Dionysia coming up, the curse would be wiped away before it had taken effect. Celeus is impressed. He would never have thought of that by himself. It's why you hire a professional if you want the job done properly.

Quickly he approves the wording and gives the sorceress the names of the other tavern owners. She will make a similar curse for each and when Celeus comes back in an hour there will be a quick sealing ritual. The tablets will be folded, and then in hen's blood and ashes Celeus will hammer a nail through them to bind the spell.

After that, the sorceress will send the spell to the Underworld. She does not like this part. Next time the moon is gone from the sky she must go unseen to the cemetery with her dread message. She will be alone in the dark, or at least she hopes she will be alone. When you invoke spirits, demons and dark goddesses on a weekly basis, you never quite know what might be waiting for you in the haunted dark. That's the other reason people come to her. If something goes wrong with a spell, it backfires on the caster of that spell, not the person who commissioned it.

There's a funeral tomorrow. That poor daughter of Alcaeus, who died at just fourteen years. The sorceress will furtively sneak into the enclosure of the girl's tomb, and there bury the lead tablets beneath the soil. At the dark of the moon, Hermes, who leads the spirits of the dead to the gates of the Underworld, will come for the girl. Drawn by secret sigils on the lead tablets, Hermes will find the message and take it to the addressees, Hekate, Hermes and – since Celeus called upon her in the presence of Mormo – the sorceress has had no choice but to also add Artemis.

Once the tablets are found and the message delivered, the curse is irrevocable. The tavern owners are doomed.

The Finished Curse

Discovered northeast of the Piraeus in the *deme* of Xypete in 2003, one of five lead tablets, folded over, with a nail driven through.

> *Hekate of the Underworld, Hermes of the Underworld,*
>   *Artemis of the Underworld*
> *Cast your hate at Phanagora and Demetrios, their taverns,*
>   *their property and all they possess*
> *I, the enemy of Phanagora and Demetrios bind them in blood*
>   *and ashes with all the dead*
> *The coming four-year cycle will not release you, for I bind you,*
>   *Demetrios,*
> *In the strongest of bonds, with a kynotos on your tongue.*

FOLLOWING TRANS. OF J. L. LAMONT 'A NEW COMMERCIAL
CURSE TABLET FROM CLASSICAL ATHENS' *ZEITSCHRIFT FUR
PAPYROLOGIE UND EPIGRAPHIK* 196, 159–174 (2015)

THE WRESTLING INSTRUCTOR PREPARES A CLASS

I n Athens, exercise is a serious business. Ariston the wrestling instructor likes to remind the class of the time when Socrates reproved a friend called Epigenes for being out of shape:

The fit are healthy and strong … they live a better, more pleasant life and leave a better inheritance for their children … In all uses of the body it is vital that you keep it working as efficiently as possible. Even when you are thinking, a process which seems hardly to concern the body at all, everyone knows that bad mistakes are often due to poor health. The unfit are prone to memory loss. Depression, melancholia, and even insanity can attack the mind so powerfully as to drive all knowledge from it. Nothing protects a man like a fit and healthy body …

Anyway, it is disgraceful that through indolence you might age without ever seeing what you might have become if you had allowed your body to reach its full potential in strength and beauty. Are you so inattentive that you can't see that this won't happen all by itself? [9]

Socrates is often at odds with his fellow Athenians, but on this topic the philosopher, the wrestling instructor Ariston and the city are totally in agreement. So much so that Athens has not one very substantial gymnasium, but three. (There are also several minor gymnasia, some used as private training grounds for professional athletes.) Apart from the Academy where Ariston works, there is also the Lyceum and the Cynosarges.

These gymnasia are located outside the city walls because track and field exercises need a lot of space. The Cynosarges, in the southern suburbs, is the least fashionable. The other two gymnasia are for citizens only, so the children of mixed parentage exercise here, as do illegitimate children. Doubtless this discrimination engenders a certain bitterness, so it is unsurprising that the Cynic school of philosophy developed at the Cynosarges.

The names of the Academy and Lyceum are associated with learning because the Greeks in general, and the Athenians in particular, do not separate the education of the body from the training of the mind. Gymnasia are not afterthoughts attached to schools – they are the schools. Every morning, boys troop to each of the various gymnasia to receive a rigorous physical and mental workout. Instructors at the gymnasium each promote their speciality. Ariston does wrestling, Socrates wants instructors to concentrate on music; others prefer dance.

The boys have little choice about attending. They are sent by their fathers, and for the first third of the day only instructors

No gymnastic exercise can equal [dance] for beauty and overall development of agility, flexibility, and pure strength. The art does everything – it sharpens intellects, it exercises the body, and delights the spectator, while teaching history [through the ancient art].

LUCIAN *ON PANTOMIME* 72

and boys under the age of sixteen are allowed on the premises. When the gymnasium is later open to men of all ages, those who studied there as boys return to the scene. Apart from the necessity of keeping fit in a warrior culture (every able-bodied Athenian male eventually sees combat), gymnasia offer good music, scientific discourse or philosophical debate. Socrates, for example, hangs around the Lyceum and takes on all comers as he defends his personal philosophy of knowledge and the soul.

At the Academy, lessons today will start with a wrestling bout. The gymnasiarch believes that rigorous exercise first thing in the morning stimulates the brain. So firmly does this gymnasiarch believe in physical exercise that this makes up fully half the curriculum, with music and grammar taking up most of the rest. What the gymnasiarch believes is important, because the gymnasiarch – Ariston's boss – is the absolute master of his domain.

Gymnasiarchs are usually wealthy and important people. A gymnasiarch pays the expenses of the gymnasium from his own pocket – the oils used by the athletes to clean themselves, the sand of the wrestling arenas and the slaves who maintain the place. His success is measured on two counts: how many competitors he prepares for the great athletic competitions of Greece, and the education and deportment of his young charges. It's a prestigious position.

The boys have already disrobed (the word 'gymnasium' comes from the Greek for 'naked exercise'). They are protected from the public gaze both by the marble peristyle that surrounds the exercise area and by the many trees that provide shade. In fact, the groves of the Academy are famous. When

PLATO AND FRIENDS REMINISCE IN THIS MOSAIC FROM ROMAN POMPEII

school is out, a common adult leisure occupation is strolling and picnicking among the trees. All the more so now because the groves of the Academy are among the few mature trees remaining after the regular Spartan invasions of the earlier war. In their attempts to lure the Athenians out from behind their fortifications and fight, the Spartans methodically devastated everything outside the walls that they reckoned that the Athenians might value. In recognition of their ancient debt, the pious Spartans left the sacred groves of the Academy intact, but only those.

A Brief History of the Academy

Back in the mythical past of Athens, the whole of Attica was united by the often less than heroic Theseus. The lowest point came when Theseus abducted the beautiful but underage Helen of Sparta. Helen was hidden in Athens while Theseus rushed off to another adventure in the Underworld.

Theseus was not home when the vengeful Spartan army came to look for their missing princess. A man called Academus investigated, and discovered the missing child. (Helen was soon abducted again to start her career as Helen of Troy.)

In return for saving their city, the Athenians gave Academus some well-shaded land by the river. This became a gymnasium, and the haunt of philosophers. The fame of the Academy endured into subsequent eras, so today there are literally thousands of 'Academies' around the world. Meanwhile, the twenty-first-century Academy in Athens has reverted to its origins, and is again a tree-shaded park.

Ariston waits as the boys file into the *loutron*, the first room one encounters on entry into the gymnasium, and there carefully wash and oil their bodies. After wrestling, they will proceed to the *cotyceum*, where they rub themselves down with more oil and then throw carefully refined dust over the oil. This is the usual Greek form of washing. Soap is known, but used exclusively by barbarians. Who wants to go around smelling of lye all day? Instead, olive oil, soaked with sweet-smelling herbs and unguents, is allowed to seep into the pores before it and the dust are together scraped from the skin by a curved copper instrument called a strigil.

←――――――――――――――――――――――――――――――――→

I believe that the first things children sense are pleasure and pain. These are how virtue and vice first present themselves ... Now, by education, I mean training children into suitable habits which will make them instinctively virtuous ...

The particular training in respect of pleasure and pain will cause them always, from early life to its end, to hate what they ought to hate, and love what they ought to love. That training can be separated from the rest, and that is the part which I consider can be rightly called education.

PLATO *THE LAWS* BK 2.15FF

←――――――――――――――――――――――――――――――――→

Obviously, given his numerous other concerns, the gymnasiarch cannot instruct the boys in person. Two other instructors handle that. The first is the *paedotribos*, an ex-athlete who focuses on the training and diet most beneficial to young boys. It is the *paedotribos* whom the gymnasiarch consults on matters such as whether to start the boys' day with a brisk wrestling match. Today, the *paedotribos* confirms that indeed it should, so long as the wrestling is a 'stand-up' fight. The other kind involves getting down and dirty on the ground and it can get really vicious – so much so that in professional 'ground' wrestling, sometimes only one of the competitors gets up afterwards.

In a stand-up fight, the winner has to throw his opponent to the ground three times. The pairing of the boys for this contest is done by the *gymnastes*. Ariston is one of these instructors – the actual trainers who supervise the routines laid down by the *paedotribos*. To ensure that no one gets injured in the morning warm-up, Ariston sends the weakest boys to a corner of the peristyle to refine their strength and skills by wrestling with a sand-filled canvas sack that dangles from the ceiling.

The other boys are paired off so that strength and skill are matched, though sometimes a stronger boy has a more skilled opponent. This leaves the instructor with his usual problem; what to do with Aristocles. The boy cannot be left out of the morning warm-up because his parents are both noble and powerful. (The mother is a descendant of the ancient law-giver Solon, and the father of Aristocles traces his descent back yet further, to the now-extinct kings of Athens.) On the other hand, there's no one with whom the boy can be paired for a fair fight. Looking at his Herculean shoulders, it is hard to believe the boy is just twelve years old.

Not only is this broad-shouldered chunk of muscle extremely strong, he is also extremely skilled. Another boy with his physique might coast through the wrestling on strength alone. Aristocles does not. Rather he uncritically follows the dictum of Socrates that a man has a duty to himself to be as physically and mentally perfect as he can become. Aristocles has studied wrestling with the same joyless ferocity that he brings to any other physical and mental exercise. Other boys throw their opponents to the ground. Aristocles throws them halfway across the gymnasium.

Ariston is tempted to take on the boy himself. He once had something of a reputation as a wrestler in his native city of

---

Plato

Plato was born in 428 BC, making him twelve years old at the present time (though an alternative birth year of 423 is credible). His parents had close connections with the conservative, reactionary aristocrats who thoroughly disliked the Athenian democracy.

As a wrestler, young Plato was apparently good enough to compete at the prestigious Isthmian games. Once he met Socrates, he became a devoted philosopher. Plato founded his school of philosophy at the Academy where his most famous student was a young polymath called Aristotle. Later in life, Plato travelled to Syracuse in the hope of making its ruler into the philosopher-king of his dreams. The trip did not end well.

An unabashed believer in the superiority of the male Greek mind, Plato further outrages modern readers with his brutal social politics (for example, killing the mentally infirm to purify the species). Nevertheless, his various works, principally the *Laws* and the *Republic*, have laid the foundations of how western civilizations understand the world.

Argos. Young Aristocles might be a pre-adolescent, but he is almost Ariston's height and, if anything, slightly wider across the shoulders. The *gymnastes* keeps in shape through regular bouts with his colleagues, and he can't help wondering how young Aristocles would shape up against professional opposition. That won't happen, of course. Pederasty is common enough among Athenians that no sane parents would allow their naked and oiled-up child to have a grappling session with an adult, no matter how pure his motives.

The *gymnastes* solves his problem by sending one of the borderline cases to do battle with the sand sack, which leaves him with an odd number of wrestlers. The partnerless wrestler is, of course, Aristocles, who eyes the instructor with thoughtful disgruntlement, which makes plain that he knows exactly what the *gymnastes* has done, and why.

The instructor points to the three most competent pairs. 'You six. Fight to the first throw only. Whoever wins that throw gets a turn with young Plato here.'

'Plato' means 'broad' in the sense that a plateau or a mighty river is broad. It is a common nickname for those who take an extra size across the chest for tunics. With Aristocles, the name is so appropriate that few call him anything but 'Plato'.

He learned gymnastics under Ariston, the Argive wrestler. It was Ariston who gave him the name 'Plato' because of his burly build. As Alexander informs us in his Successions of Philosophers, this came to replace his original name of Aristocles, [which he was named] after his grandfather.

DIOGENES LAËRTIUS *PLATO* BK 3.1

After wrestling comes music, and Plato will do less well here. He has a rather weak, discordant voice. He makes a fair fist of poetry, and currently applies his intense focus to the specialist type called 'dithyrambs'. Being Plato, he will work at this relentlessly until he recites his poetry with a voice as sweet and delicate as a lily.[10] (Plato will later try his hand at writing tragic plays. While taking one entry to a competition he paused to listen to Socrates sounding off. Realizing how weak were his words compared to the philosopher's eloquence he cried, 'Come, God of Fire, Plato needs you now,' and burned his play on the spot.)

For now, Plato is ready to take out in advance the musical frustrations of the coming lesson. He flexes his shoulders and grins companionably at the chosen six, who start their preliminary bouts with a marked lack of enthusiasm.

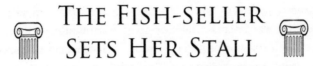

THE FISH-SELLER
SETS HER STALL

As she sets up, Alcestis sees the wool merchant from Euboea anxiously examining the sky.

'Don't worry,' she calls cheerfully. 'It won't rain!'

The wool-seller returns her smile, more out of gratitude for her understanding than in appreciation of her weather-forecasting ability. It matters not to Alcestis whether it rains. In fact, she would prefer if it did. But the wool-seller would lose a day's trade. Wool is sold by the *mina* (a weight approximating to 22 oz or 630 g) and wet wool gets heavier and therefore more expensive. Stalls in the Agora are open to the sky, so if it rains the wool gets wet, and the market authorities won't allow the wool-seller to trade at his customers' expense.

This matters more than usual today because, in the run-up to the Great Dionysia, Athens is teeming with visitors from all over the Greek world. The Agora – the city's main market area, public boulevard and social meeting space – is packed with traders from all over the Mediterranean who offer top-quality goods to the well-heeled tourist clientele. There's not a place or time in the world when stallholders have a better chance to make serious money.

The stalls opposite Alcestis run in a long row backing on to the east side of the Street of Panathena. The row stretches half a *stade* (around 84 metres or 275 feet) from the south stoa to level with the Altar of the Twelve Gods. At a glance, Alcestis can see elegant Persian slippers and gowns of Amorges wool woven so fine as to be shamelessly transparent. Another stall has a rack of red and black Italian cloaks made from the thick wool of Lucarnia, practically dripping in lanolin oil and proof against all but the heaviest shower. Then there's a stall with little pots of rare Arabian perfumes and unguents, and beside that a tradesman loads his table with stacks of papyrus while he too casts anxious looks skyward.

Alcestis recalls that yesterday someone confronted a pot-bellied little man who was fingering the fine Lycian rugs sold a few stalls down.

'Ho, Socrates! What brings you here? I thought rush mats were all you needed?'

The man straightened up, and Alcestis saw that his startlingly ugly face was alight with wonder.

'Oh, I come here often,' Socrates had said, waving an arm that encompassed the rows of stalls in their entirety. 'I am constantly amazed at how many things I actually don't need.'

Well, thinks Alcestis as she sets another hunk of fish on its bed of beet leaves, he doesn't need my fish, that's for sure. He's a smelt-fish eater, I'll bet. An anchovy or salt-fish man.

That's an insult but, unlike the rest of Athens, Socrates doesn't care what fish he eats. Some societies have wine snobs, others judge people by jewellery, clothing or footwear. But footwear hardly matters when even wealthy Athenians often go barefoot, so the city's folk judge each other by their taste in fish. Small fish, such as sprats and anchovies, are eaten by those who cannot afford better, and by Socrates, who can. Squid is acceptable at any table, and the wealthy look for the best cuts of tuna, grey-head or other large fish.

Several stalls offer such gastronomic delicacies, yet when the bell rings to open the market, the first rush will be to the stall of Alcestis the Syracusan. She sells Messinan eels. It is generally agreed that the prince of fish, the pinnacle of oesophageal delight, is the eel. As the playwright remarks, 'If I were a god, not a sacrifice would I allow on my altar, unless it came with an eel.' A regular eel is served with reverence on special occasions. Yet the eel guaranteed to make the server's social reputation at any dinner is the fish-snob's golden fleece, the Messinan.

'That you can put such food to your lips, citizen of Messinia, privileges you above other mortal men ... that Eel is the lord of the feast, master of the culinary battlefield.' So wrote Archestratus in his famous poem *The Gastronome*, and Athenians enthusiastically agree. When Messinan eels become available Athenians literally fall over themselves to pay silly prices for them. The runners-up are eels from the lakes of Boeotia but, delicious as these eels are, they lack the Messinan cachet of acute scarcity.

Which is why, fifteen days ago in Sicily, Alcestis and her husband loaded *Thetis*, their little trading ship, with Syracusan cheeses, amphorae of dark, heavy Sicilian wine and above all, barrels of Messinan eels – some salted, some smoked, and some live and twining sinuously at the bottom of the salt-water casks. Alcestis has been selling at the Agora for three days now, deliberately keeping the eel in short supply, so those elegant horse-breeding idiots with their bottomless purses think themselves lucky for the chance to pay her five days' wages for a single serving.

It is interesting that meat is less popular in the city, despite the huge meat-laden feasts enjoyed by the heroes of

Homer's poetry. One reason is that most Athenians get meat through sacrifice. Through an ancient bargain with the gods, the deity receives the life of the sacrificial beast and the skin, bones and horns (if any). Humans get the meat. Yet because of the communal nature of sacrifice, all involved get an equal share. So meat allocated after a sacrifice is usually a hunk of flesh, innards and gristle, hacked out of the carcass with little regard to the location of the best or even most suitable cuts.

Furthermore, there's the matter of image. Most fish is sold in the markets of the Agora or Piraeus, so fish is essentially an urban dish. Those out in the country have beards greasy with pork fat. The city sophisticate dines delicately on white, flaky fish.

Today is the last day that Alcestis will set her stall. She has advertised the fact and expects to be sold out within the hour. Thereafter, she will spend the day haggling for goods that will make her a profit back home: bolts of silk, vials of purple Tyrian dye – the only colour-fast dye in the known world – Athenian vases and, hopefully, an advance script of the new work by Euripides. The playwright is hugely revered in Syracuse and a first edition of his latest work will go for a fortune.

The Athenian and Eastern merchants in the Agora will scowl at the indignity of dealing directly with a woman. No respectable female east of the Peloponnese would dream of bargaining in the market. Alcestis has seen, and secretly despises, aristocratic Athenian women so swaddled in veils that they are practically walking tents. Their purchases are made by servants into whose ears the women discreetly mutter. Alcestis does her business personally, and does it well.

Let the traders blanch at her naked face. Soon enough they'll be looking at the silver in her hand. They also know that a woman so uninhibited in her appearance will be every bit as shameless in demanding the lowest price – and she'll get it. Alcestis has spent

A FISH-SELLER AND HIS CUSTOMER

the first part of the week researching her fellow stallholders. She knows the break-even sale point of every item she's after.

Her husband would do the job, but he's at the Piraeus getting *Thetis* ready to sail, with an olive-branch club and two hired dockyard thugs to protect the cargo already in the hold. Apart from the perils of the port, there's still the fraught journey back to Italy. After a gentle voyage past Aegina towards Corinth, there's the Peloponnese and the terrifying tack around the deadly promontory of Cape Malea.

Then the little merchantman will run up towards Corcyra, hugging the coast while the crew pray to avoid the sleek Luburnian pirate vessels that sneak down the coast from Albania. Then, provided no late spring storms wreck the ship on its sprint across the Adriatic to the Italian port of Brundisium, Alcestis can look forward to a leisurely cruise down the craggy coastline. A quick hop across the strait of Messina, en route offering the region's patron god, Zeus Ithomatas, a libation in thanks for all the eels. Then home to haven in Ortygia, the main port of Syracuse.

Now the crowds gather at the rope barrier that holds back customers until the market is formally open. Alcestis completes her preparation by setting a little stack of weights next to the balance she obtained from the Agoranomists. Agoranomists oversee the market from their offices in the Stoa of Zeus, which is appropriate enough as Zeus is the god of order.

To ensure that goods are sold in true measure, market weights must conform to the official standard. Woe betide the trader who is accused before the Agoranomists if his weights are placed in the balance and found wanting. Regular stallholders have weights stamped with a little owl (the semi-official seal of Athens) to show that they – literally – measure up. Visitors such as Alcestis find it easier to rent the entire set from the market authorities. That way, if disgruntled customers complain about getting short weight she can simply refer them to the officials in the stoa.

Thinking of this, Alcestis looks briefly over her shoulder at the olive-oil dealer in the row behind. On the first day that she was at the Agora that stallholder was accused of selling short measures. The oil seller does not have a set of weights and measures because his high-legged table has a succession of bowls embedded in the surface. At the bottom of the bowl is a tap.

So when someone wants – for example – 12 *kyathoi* of oil (just over half a litre or just under a US pint), the dealer pours the amount into that bowl and when the bowl is filled, he opens the tap at the bottom into whatever container the customer provides. On this occasion a customer had suspected that the line that marks a 'full' bowl had been drawn lower than it should be.

Two market officials had come marching out of the stoa, their way cleared by one of the burly Scythian bowmen who keeps order in the Agora. The officials carried a vase with markings up the side. This they solemnly filled with oil to the precise 12 *kyathoi* mark and then poured it into the stallholder's bowl. The result proved that, if anything, the stallholder had been over-generous – the full measure of oil came short of the marking by a finger's width.

'I am the market-inspector,' said Pythias. 'If you have come to shop for food, let me help you.'

'Thanks, but no. I've already purchased fish for supper.'

Pythias took my basket and shook it around to examine the fish more thoroughly. 'How much did you pay for these sprats?' he enquired.

'It took some bargaining, but I beat the man down to twenty copper coins.'

Outraged by this information, he pulled me back to the Agora by my hand. 'Which of these vendors sold you that trash?' he demanded.

Once I had pointed out the little old man as he squatted in his corner, Pythias descended on him in the full wrath of his office. 'You rogue – how dare you cheat a friend so mercilessly … I will show you how villains such as yourself are kept in their place while I'm in charge here!'

He emptied the basket on the ground, and ordered one of his attendants to trample the fish into paste. After this, he smiled, content with the rigour with which he had fulfilled his duties. 'That is punishment enough, Lucius,' he said. 'We have shamed the old scoundrel.'

He waved at me to depart, which I did, stunned and speechless, without my dinner or money to buy another.

'PUNISHING' A FISH-TRADER, APULEIUS *THE GOLDEN ASS* 1.25

Alcestis uses a handful of thin, straight twigs to keep the ever-present flies off her fish, so as the market opens they look fresh and ready. Yet the first customer does not buy at once.

Instead he looks over her products and opines loudly, 'I would watch that smoked eel. The other night young Chryshippos ate eel like that, and has not been off the privy since. As to the fresh, they do say fresh eel should not be eaten before June. It affects the bodily humours.'

Alcestis eyes the loudmouth. 'I have salted eel also,' she remarks. The man recoils, beard twitching in agitation.

'Not the salted! Why, the last salted eel I ate was almost all salt. Afterwards I drank so much water I was in danger of becoming a fish myself. Indeed, I can still taste that salt, though I never recall being able to taste the fish.'

'Tell me,' an unamused Alcestis enquires, 'does that old trick still work on anyone? You stand back and badmouth the product until a naive stallholder either drops her prices or offers you a discount to go away. That's not working. Either you buy now, at full price, or I swear by Hermes, the god of merchants, you do not buy at all from me. Not even if I take everything home unsold.'

The two match stare for stare, while other buyers watch the stand-off. Finally, the loudmouth says, unabashed, 'In that case, I'll take those two sections of smoked eel over there, if you please.'

Alcestis briskly prepares the order, but before handing it over she says, 'Oh, and there's a critic's fee of three obols. Cough up, or this fish goes to the gentleman behind you for a half-drachma discount.'

Without hesitation, the former critic uses his tongue to dig the surcharge from his mouth. Athenian coins are tiny.

An obol is half the size of a fingernail and weighs very little. A coin-purse makes one a walking invitation to theft, and Athenian tunics have no pockets. So the easiest way to carry the tiny coins is to slip them between gums and lip into the little pouches that nature seems to have designed for the purpose.

Without comment, Alcestis drops the coins into the saucer of water that serves as her cash register. Then the rush is on, with customers elbowing each other aside, each furiously trying to outbid his neighbour. Prices soar as the stock diminishes and, as predicted, the table is cleared in under an hour.

Alcestis is cleaning up her stall when a perspiring middle-aged man rushes over. 'The eel! Is there any eel left? Any at all?'

They'll bring baskets of eels ... and we will all rush to buy them, squabbling for possession with Morychus, Teleas, Glaucetes and every other glutton. When Melanthius comes to market last of all, they'll tell him. 'Sorry, no eels. They're sold out.'

And he will groan and start into that monologue of his from Medea. 'Alas, I perish, I'm dying. Oh, woe, that I have let those hidden in the beet leaves escape from me!'

ARISTOPHANES *THE PEACE* L.1002

Alcestis shakes her head. The man stands, gasping. He has evidently rushed here as fast as he could from whatever delayed him. 'You know me, don't you? Melanthius, the tragic playwright. I'm famous. You must have something set aside for special customers. I'll pay double.' The playwright starts digging desperately through the beet leaves on Alcestis' table in the hope of finding an overlooked fillet.

He stops at the sound of a snigger from behind him. A well-dressed young man with a sallow complexion stands there smirking. Melanthius throws up his hands in horror. 'Aristophanes, no! I've lost my eels, and you're going to tell the world. You wouldn't, would you? Not even you ...!'

THE VISITOR SAVES
A LIFE

Two men leave the Agora. They are deep in discussion, though the conversation is periodically interrupted by enjoyment of the honey-and-apple pastries that the pair purchased at a stall as they were leaving. Passers-by glance curiously at the two, for the older man is clearly the student. He listens attentively, and periodically stops as he commits some detail to memory.

This surprises many, for Phoikos is a respected physician with students of his own. The younger man – a burly fellow in his mid-forties – is a stranger. His accent has the sing-song rhythm that marks citizens of the eastern Aegean. (In many eastern cities Attic Greek has mutated into different dialects. Indeed, so error-prone has become the speech of citizens of Soli in Asia Minor that serious grammatical errors will for evermore be called 'solecisms'.) This is Hippocrates of Kos – a man who accepts his title as the world's greatest doctor without false modesty, but as a simple statement of fact.

'It's the whole body,' Hippocrates is saying. 'When you think on it, when the lungs have a fever, is not the brain also somewhat disordered? A cut on the hand can lead to a bloody flux from the bowel. A fat belly is a sign that the person carrying that belly will die sooner, of whatever causes, than he would if he were slim.

'That's the issue, you understand, which I have with the school at Knidos. If there's a problem with the liver, they treat the liver, as if the liver was not, one might say, part of a community of organs within the body. I have observed that problems with the liver can become problems with the skin, and also the kidneys. A tumour starts in one part of the body, but the roots go deep elsewhere. You have to treat the body as a whole.'

Phoikos digs a shred of apple from between his teeth. So a rogue tumour must be excised, before it spreads to and damages other organs – he must pass that analogy to his friend Nicias. An adept politician and orator, Nicias will enjoy working the words of Hippocrates into a speech condemning his rival, Alcibiades.

Phoikos shares Nicias' opinion that young Alcibiades is their city's tumour. A corruption of the body politic with his waywardness, his reckless behaviour, and his disrespect for his elders and for the gods.

Alcibiades is an outstanding candidate for ostracism. Athenians can vote to exile a politician for ten years. Not for anything illegal, but because the citizens judge him to be a danger to the body politic.

Nicias could argue that Alcibiades should be ostracized, just as doctors excise a tumour before it damages the rest of its host. The medical analogy might help explain this to the people. Phoikos is convinced that Alcibiades has to be exiled before he drags Athens into that dangerous and stupid Sicilian expedition.

It suddenly occurs to Phoikos that he has completely lost track of what Hippocrates has been saying for the last minute. He is saved from admitting this by a man in a dishevelled tunic who pushes through the crowd. 'Phoikos! Has anyone seen the doctor? He left the Agora by this street. I seek Phoikos!'

'I am he.'

'Come, please, at once. There's been an accident. A column drum fell on someone.'

The man seeking help is hopping from one foot to another in impatience. 'It's the temple of Hephaestion – we're doing repairs. The drum slipped off a cart. Young Deculion, it's lying on his leg. So you'll help him?'

This question is addressed to the backs of the two doctors. They have already taken off down the street at a dead run and arrive just in time to stop the workmen from killing their patient.

The men have wedged wooden poles under the column drum and are preparing to lever it off an inert body on the cobblestones. Nearby, a pair of oxen hitched to a cart have been joined by a crowd who offer comment, prayer and advice in equal measure.

Phoikos pauses to suck in air. Meanwhile, Hippocrates unceremoniously shoves the workmen away from the poles and kicks aside the person bent over the victim, whose abdomen he then cautiously palpates.

'Breathing shallow, pulse thready. Skin pallid and clammy. There's a large contusion and swelling at the back of the skull. No depression and the bone is unbroken. Was this man hit on the head?'

'I don't know. He went down hard,' says one of the workmen. 'Must have caught his head a crack on the cobbles.

He's not moved or spoken since. But isn't that column drum the main problem? We've got to get it off him.'

Columns such as those at the front of this temple are not carved from single blocks of stone. Most columns are two or three times the height of a man, and even finding suitable stone to make into such monoliths would be hard work. Instead, the average column is made of 'drums' – circular lumps of stone around a cubit high, and flat on the top and bottom. Some have holes in the flat surfaces where metal rods can be used to secure the stone to drums above and below. Mostly, though, the sheer weight of a column drum holds it in place.

BATTLEFIELD REPAIRS

Once all the drums have been joined into a column, workmen put cement paste mixed with powdered stone into the gaps and sand it down so that the joins are indistinguishable from the rest of the stone. The drum lying across young Deculion's lower leg is intended for the base of one such column and is a hefty lump of marble.

Hippocrates explains, 'Remove that drum and the boy's death will be quick and certain, instead of highly probable, as is now the case. The rush of blood into the damaged limb upsets the body humours, see? But act as you wish. A swift death might be doing the lad a favour, it's true, but if you do it, he can't be my patient. The fundamental principle of my school is, "First, do no harm."'

The workman looks at Phoikos. 'Who in Hades is this?'

'Hippocrates of Kos. Only the greatest doctor of our age. He has travelled in Egypt and Babylon, and knows more of medicine than ten of me combined. I would call this the boy's lucky day – except that it evidently isn't. If you want to save him, do whatever Hippocrates says – and don't take offence. He can be a bit abrupt.'

Hippocrates ignores the character reference given by his companion. 'The leg has got to go.' He indicates the mangled flesh between column drum and roadway. 'Actually, it has gone already. We must treat it as though it is a case of gangrene and remove it below the joint. Phoikos, take notes – even if this patient dies, the documentation will be useful.'

'That's fairly heartless,' remarks a spectator. Hippocrates looks up.

'Life is brief, but the art of medicine endures. What would be heartless would be to stand by and do nothing to help this boy, nor learn so as to later help others. Standing by in ignorance is exactly what you are doing, you understand?

Until you become no worse than useless, be still and hold your tongue.'

Hippocrates turns to his fellow doctor. 'Phoikos, I shall cut here, where the nerves are already severed. It is living flesh, and cutting that is not advised. If the patient is awake, he will

Hippocrates

When we talk of a person convalescing, or relapsing, or whether a disease is acute, chronic or an epidemic, we are using terms categorized by Hippocrates, the 'Father of Medicine'.

Hippocrates firmly established medicine as a science apart from religion and theurgy. (Theurgy is the use of supernatural means to effect a cure, such as prayer, magical amulets and sacrifices.)

Hippocrates established scientific principles of observation, clinical diagnosis and protocols for medical procedures. The amputation described here is lifted directly from the 'Hippocratic corpus' – texts written by Hippocrates (allegedly) and his successors at the medical school that he founded on his birth island of Kos. 'First, do no harm' is still incorporated into the Hippocratic Oath taken by many modern doctors. Another quote – sometimes rendered as '*Ars longa, vita brevis*' and translated along the lines of 'Art endures, life is short' – has been kidnapped by the literary types, but was first applied to the art of medicine.

Hippocrates was at least eighty years old when he died, and some accounts have him living past a hundred. His name means 'the strength of horses' and, metabolically speaking, that was the case.

quickly pass out and probably never revive. Our patient is unconscious and probably going to die anyway, so we must attempt it. What is the main danger here?'

'Haemorrhage?'

'Indeed. Large blood vessels have been severed, and the bone is crushed. Usually with a leg this mangled, I would wait and let gangrene separate the bone as a natural process. After all, suppurating flesh is harder to look at than to treat. Yet we can't do that here, you understand, and some haemorrhage at the crisis is useful, for it flushes ill humours from the site of injury. What remedy for haemorrhage do you suggest?'

'Burning?'

'Possible, indeed possible. Desperate situations require desperate measures. Yet I shall first try compression. I have seen patients recover, even when gangrene takes a leg at the femur. I need ...' Hippocrates rolls up his eyes as he searches his memory. 'Water. Clean water, mind you, some warm and some hot potfuls of water. Vinegar. Honey. Fig leaves. Pine resin. And I need cloth – clean linen. Get it from the market. A knife, as sharp as possible, the blade rust-free. And leather – about so.' Hippocrates holds up two hands making a circle with a gap of about two inches between his fingertips. 'Carthaginian leather, if you can find it. Otherwise any leather, stretched thin.'

'For what do you intend the leather?' asks Phoikos curiously.

'I shall do a wedge resection here.' Hippocrates traces an inverted 'V' just below the patient's knee, having to dig his fingers under the drum at the tips of the V. 'See the bump in the leg there? The bone is shattered, so the least flesh is that which we leave here at the point of the V. We pull the longer flaps of flesh together below the bone, cup the stump in the leather and compress with bandages. The leather causes the flesh to bind to itself and not to the cloth.'

Hippocrates prods the point just below the broken bone, and looks to see if the patient flinches. There is no movement.

'We need that knife now!' Hippocrates bellows, causing some in the crowd to start back in surprise. Looking down at the patient he mutters. 'In the first place, diagnosis. What is right and what is out of place. What is obvious, and what is needed to be known. What may be learned by visual examination, then by touch, then by hearing. Even smell and taste can convey information. Then understanding the data, without which all the other observations are pointless. Done that.

'Next we need clarity. About the patient, who is in charge of the operation, what instruments are available, what light. We must be clear how many things are to be done, what they are and in what order we will do them. I should be *here*, for the light is common sunlight, and it falls on the operating area *so*. My garment does not interfere with the operation. My fingernails are trimmed. My assistant is reasonably competent. We now need the instruments, laid out and in order of use. You, Phoikos, will pass them to me. Have them ready beforehand and do as I direct.'

Beyond Hippocrates the bystanders have leapt into action. If there has to be a crisis, Athens is a good venue to have it. Athenians react quickly and coolly in emergencies, perhaps because of their unfortunate habit of provoking such emergencies in the first place. Within minutes Hippocrates has his materials. A razor-sharp skinning knife is in his hands, and behind him the leader of the work gang bickers with the stallholder who provided the linen.

'You two – hold the boy's shoulders. He will probably

stay unconscious, mind you, but I don't want him jumping around like a landed trout if he feels the knife. Phoikos, we need temporary compression here, at the adductor magnus. There's a major artery between the tibia and fibia, and when I cut that, you need to suppress the blood in the femoral artery. I have seen the Egyptians do this. It is like damming a river upstream before you breach a dyke below. It works, anyway. You press there and the bleeding here will be reduced until we have closed and compressed the wound.'

'Why not simply leave the compression on the thigh, if it is so effective?' enquires Phoikos.

'Doesn't work, you understand? Tie a bandage or ligature too tight and for some reason the lower part mortifies and eventually rots. That's why even with compression below the knee, we will eventually do it with the weight of bandages rather than their tightness.'

Hippocrates works smoothly, occasionally flipping the knife to separate muscle fibres with the slender handle instead of slicing through them with the blade. He doesn't really need Phoikos, which is just as well, because Phoikos is occupied with jamming a knuckle into the upper leg at the point Hippocrates has indicated.

When he stops to ease a cramped elbow, Phoikos causes a rush of blood over the surgical site and a string of irritated obscenities from Hippocrates. Phoikos now shifts so he can keep the pressure reassuringly constant. The other workmen have appointed themselves as human barriers against the press of a gathering crowd, straining for a closer look at the operation in progress.

'Leather,' demands Hippocrates. He examines with disgust the thin sheet he is handed. 'Is this from the curtain of a privy door? While I irrigate the wound with vinegar, scrub that leather down, smear the cleanest side lightly with honey. It will have to do.

'Now, this bandage we shape like a cup, and sit it over the leather-covered stump, so.[11] The honey helps to prevent infection, though expect plentiful pus as the wound heals. It will need draining later.

'Now we wrap the wound firmly, because you understand there should be absolutely no swelling at this point. We start here, and wrap so that the next layer of wrapping holds the lower one in place. The incisions are at the left and right, so the top and bottom of each circuit get a dab of resin – here and here. That stops the bandage slipping. Oh, and now remove that column drum. It's in the way.'

Amputations

The ancient Athenians, like most ancient Greeks, forbade the practice of dissection. Most anatomical knowledge was obtained through examining human leftovers opened on the battlefield by enthusiastic amateurs with swords.

While it was understood that cleanliness helped to prevent infection, the Greeks were ignorant of what caused infection, and sterilization of medical instruments did not happen. Consequently, major limbs were seldom amputated unless in circumstances as exceptional as those described here. Usually, the limb was kept, no matter how damaged. Often the limb would become gangrenous and drop off of its own accord, which was the preferred option. How many survived this process is unknown.

Hippocrates stands and arches his back to get rid of the kinks. He turns to the leader of the workmen and explains that either the boy will wake within the hour or not at all. Until sundown, they are to give him only sips of water to drink. Thereafter, his usual doctor can treat him as he would any wounded hoplite after a battle. Hippocrates instructs them to change the bandages after three days, and repeat until the wound has stopped weeping. If it suppurates, they need to cut away any rotten flesh that appears above the knee, and eventually the bones below will separate from the knee. For the first five days the young man is to lie flat with the stump slightly raised. Once the bleeding has stopped and the swelling has subsided, he will be allowed to sit.

Hippocrates points to a vase, and Phoikos pours warm water over Hippocrates bloody hands. Hippocrates shrugs off the effusive thanks of the workers. 'Obviously, my colleague needs to be paid for his time. As to mine, consider this a gift from me to one of the citizens of Athens.' (Unlike Phoikos, Hippocrates is independently wealthy. For him, medicine really is a calling rather than a job.)

Hippocrates pauses, wiping down his arms with cloth left over from the linen bandages. 'Mind you,' he tells the foreman, 'there is something you can do for us. While we clean up, send someone down to the pastry stall in the Agora, the one near the exit by the Mint. Our honey-and-apple pastries went missing somewhere along the way. Will you get us two more apiece?'

THE HOUSEWIFE
MEETS HER LOVER

A visitor to Athens might expect that the wife of a high-ranking government official would be exempt from menial household tasks such as fetching water. But that's because most visitors can't understand how Athenian democracy functions. In most places city councillors are well-connected, wealthy aristocrats. In Athens, councillors need only be male, citizens and have a pulse.

The Athenians rotate civic duties, so almost every male citizen holds public office at least once in his life. There are 500 seats on the boule (the steering body for the Athenian Assembly), and members are rotated out every year. Membership is not renewable and a person serves only once. A serving member of the boule is an important person. He is usually also seconded to one of the many committees that oversee the day-to-day running of the city, supervising other state officials, and making sure that monies allocated to the navy and public buildings, for example, are properly spent.

Tymale's husband is on a committee that prepares resolutions on foreign policy. These resolutions are presented to the Assembly, debated and – if successful – voted into law. So, although a lower-middle-class estate manager by profession, right now the husband of Tymale has an important role in shaping Athenian policy. While he is doing that, Tymale is fetching water.

An Athenian household gets through a fair bit of water through cleaning, cooking and washing. While homes of the wealthy have fountains in the courtyard, the general population is supplied by spring water diverted to public water-houses. No sane person draws water from the Eridanus, the little stream that becomes an open sewer as soon as it enters the city. It is not even suitable for cattle.

Fetching water is a task Tymale shares with the household's only servant. Truth be told, though the hydria vases used to carry the water are punishingly heavy, Tymale rather enjoys the chore. It gets her out of the house. Her husband would prefer Tymale to be a proper lady whose world stops at the front door of the house. She should leave the premises only for occasional religious festivals or be escorted – heavily veiled and guarded – to other households to socialize with fellow wives.

Fortunately, a lack of household womanpower means that Tymale has to shop, dispose of waste and, of course, fetch water. So she and Photuis, her servant, stand in line with their empty hydrias at the Enneacrunos fountain. Perhaps because it springs from below the temple of Demeter, the blessed water of the Enneacrunos is always sweet and pure. The line is short today, barely stretching past the statue of Dionysus at the Odeon.

Generations ago, the process of filling hydria at the Enneacrunos was made simpler by Psistratos, the tyrant of Athens, who funnelled the spring into nine separate outlets.

At her chosen outlet, Tymale takes the opportunity to gossip with friends who were also filling their hydrias.

Their news reflects the limited world of a 'proper' Athenian housewife: the progress of weaving projects and the development of another girl's pregnancy. Tymale was recently at the Agora, and she recounts to her envious friends the different perfumes, jewellery and fabrics on offer.

As she has done for years, Tymale sprinkles fresh vine leaves across the surface of the water in her vase, then lifts the heavy container on to her head in one smooth, practised motion. (The vine leaves keep the water cool, and keep dust and grit off the surface.) The servant girl does the same. The girl seems fully restored to health. A few days ago, she ate something that violently disagreed with her. This forced Tymale to make two trips to the fountain – unescorted.

Now, as they approach the house, Tymale says, 'Photuis, when we get home, pour your water into the cistern. Then I shall give you coin for food. I need eggs, cheese and olives. Get the eggs from Alithe, the woman who keeps chickens in her garden – she sells at a discount. Get a round of goat's cheese from the stall of Diophanes by the heroon of Menestheus. My husband likes that cheese.'

The servant girl makes a sour face, which Tymale ignores. Getting the shopping from two diverse locations will take until at least the midday meal, and delay the servant's other duties. Tymale is unsympathetic. For two hours, with her husband at the boule and her servant across town, Tymale will be alone in the house. Or not. If the handsome stranger is true to his word, she will have company. Wonderful, illicit company.

She wonders who he is, this golden youth with his careless manner and easy charm. Rich, beyond doubt, for his tunic was

**TERRACOTTA STATUETTE OF AN
ATHENIAN WOMAN**

of fine fabric, with little golden grasshoppers embroidered on the hem. And utterly shameless to have approached her alone in the alley as she had returned from the fountain.

Another woman might have screamed, but perhaps not. As they say in Athens, the most respectable woman is she who is not spoken of, in either praise or blame. No woman wants to attract attention. Yet Tymale had not merely failed to scream, she had responded enthusiastically to the stranger's advances. It was the most exciting thing that had happened in years, and Tymale is bored.

Like many an Athenian girl, she was married at age fifteen to a man over twice her age. As husbands go, he is a good man, she supposes. Because Tymale's family is distantly related to the aristocratic Philaidae clan, her husband had accepted a lower dowry, which was important for a family looking to marry off a third daughter.

Tymale shares her husband's bed, and his unenthusiastic love-making. After three barren years it is disappointingly clear that conceiving a child will be a slow, uncertain business, and Tymale does so want a child. She admits to herself that this is partly because rearing a daughter will be something to do apart from endless weaving, cooking and housework with only the sullen Photuis for company.

Her husband is usually home late – often after dark – and eats supper in silence before the pair retire to bed. Tymale is sure that her husband has a mistress, someone nearer his own age who provides the conversation and company that she cannot. But he does not beat her and he gives her a generous allowance for household expenses, so Tymale can consider herself lucky. Except that's not how she feels.

Well, now someone is interested in her and – she shivers at the wanton thought – very interested in her body. When unmarried, she was often enough told that she was very pretty, though until she met the golden stranger she had never dreamed that anyone would be impudent enough to say that to a married woman.

With lively anticipation, she looks up and down the street. No one is there. In the Limnai district where she lives the streets are narrow and winding, so Tymale consoles herself that the stranger may be lurking just out of sight. She waits impatiently as Photuis opens the heavy front door and steps into the small courtyard.

She imagines how the stranger would see the courtyard, and frowns. There's a small shrine in one corner with wilting flowers, and in the other corner a fly-covered patch of dirt where her husband recently sacrificed a goat (the meat was tough and stringy). A large amphora catches rainwater off the tiled roof, and basic household implements hang from another wall.

The only greenery is from the shaded upstairs balcony where Tymale has trained vines to grow down the wall. The vines are in poor shape because Tymale has the habit of gardening bareheaded. Her husband has repeatedly reproved her for this because a tan makes her look like a harlot. So if Tymale is more than a few minutes outdoors tending to her vines, Photuis tells on her.

Entering the house, there's a roomy area to her left with two couches and a long, low table. That's where her husband dines on the rare occasions when he receives guests. Usually they eat in the smaller room which doubles as the kitchen. Tymale goes up a narrow flight of steps; their bedroom is on the left, beside the wooden door that marks the single room rather grandly called the *Gynaikeion*, or woman's quarters.

The room is well-lit from the large windows that open on to the balcony. It is dominated by a large upright loom where Tymale, assisted by Photuis, spends much of her day weaving. A large untreated mass of wool in the corner waits for Photuis to dunk it into the tub (another use for household water). Then she'll card it and eventually make a large ball that Tymale will weave into a gorgeous cloak. There's a tangle of woollen thread on the floor right now, because Tymale got the weave wrong several layers back, and had to unpick her way back to the mistake.

Tymale picks up a discarded drop spindle. The Athenians have not invented the spinning wheel, so thread is spun by attaching a circular clay weight to the bottom of a short wooden rod. Tie raw wool to the weight (called a whorl), spin it just so, and the weight stretches the wool into thread that wraps itself around the spindle. It takes practice to get woollen thread just right, but Tymale has practised for years and years. Now she spins the whorl with expert flicks of her wrist, never taking her eyes off the front gate of the courtyard.

'Some god breathed into my heart the thought that I should set up a great loom in my hall and begin weaving a robe. The web I wove was the finest wool, and very wide. When it was ready I immediately spoke, saying, "Young men who woo me, be patient."[12] Should I be patient, Penelope?'

The soft voice is almost in Tymale's ear. She jumps and whirls, the spindle dropping unheeded to the floor. The golden stranger is right behind her, smiling. 'Oh! How did you get in here?'

The stranger grins. 'Up the back wall from the alley, a quick journey across the rooftop, and I dropped on to the balcony. I've been waiting here for so long, pining for you.'

Apart from her husband, Tymale has never been so close to a man. Even in winter her husband always has the sour smell of slightly rancid sweat. This man has the deep, milky scent of sandalwood, and the muscles of his chest and abdomen feel firm and defined under her questing hand. Tymale feels as wicked as the legendary Clytemnestra betraying her husband Agamemnon, but it's a good feeling.

'Come on,' she urges, 'we don't have that long.'

Teasing, the stranger holds back. 'But what about your husband? Should he return and catch us in the act, he might, as the law permits, slay me on the spot.'

The thought of her elderly spouse assaulting anything more formidable than a plateful of beans makes Tymale giggle.

Against the muscular youth, her husband would have no chance.

'You should worry more about radishes,' she grins.

A traditional punishment for adulterers in Athens – which the sheltered Tymale naturally has never seen – is for the male adulterer to be hauled into the Agora, and have the hairs burned off his testicles with hot ash. Then he is sodomized with a radish in a punishment called *rhaphanidosis*. Not only is this extremely painful for the victim, but it can cause lasting injury.

What if he should have a radish shoved up his backside ... and then have hot ashes rip off his hair? What defence can he to offer to keep his anus from gaping?

ARISTOPHANES *THE CLOUDS* 1083–1104

Seduction is worse than rape

LYSIAS *ON THE MURDER OF ERATOSTHENES* 32–33 [13]

Yet the stranger is not discouraged. Tymale is mildly impressed, but not surprised at the ease with which he shucks her out of her chiton. He seems somebody who has had a lot of practice. Nevertheless, it's her prettiest garment. She chose that dress to impress and doesn't want it crumpled on the wooden floor. She hooks it over the frame of the loom and gently lowers herself to the floor. Then she looks back over her shoulder and waits expectantly.

Seduction, Athenian lawyers have argued, is a greater crime than rape. With a rape the injury is passing, but seduction risks permanently alienating a woman from her husband. These lawyers are, of course, Athenian males. They are unlikely to personally experience the trauma of rape, but often obsess about disloyal wives.

A married Athenian male can legally sleep with prostitutes, or have a long-term affair with whomsoever he likes, so long as she is not a female Athenian citizen of good standing. An Athenian woman, however, commits 'adultery' if she so much as kisses a man who is not her husband – even if she is unmarried. By those standards Tymale is currently committing adultery. Which is why she has positioned herself so she can immediately see anyone entering via the courtyard door.

Courtesans for pleasure, concubines for bodily urges, wives for legitimate children.

Categorizing women, Demosthenes

Afterwards, she splashes scented water into a bowl so that they can clean and generally tidy themselves up. Again, her lover is impressively practised and speedy. He is dressed and ready to go before Tymale has even picked up her chiton. He throws a last look around the room for anything compromising left behind and, ignoring Tymale, moves quickly to the balcony.

He has already chinned himself to one of the rafters when she asks, 'Will I see you again?' Tymale really does not know what answer she wants to hear. The stranger lowers himself for a moment, and she notes the impressive bulge of his tanned biceps. His smile is angelic.

'No,' he says. And he is gone.

Extracts from the *Life of Alcibiades*, Plutarch

8.9 Hipparete was a decorous and affectionate wife. However she was deeply upset by her husband [Alcibiades] consorting with lovers both Athenian and foreign. Therefore she walked out on him and moved in with her brother. Alcibiades was unperturbed and kept up his wanton ways. In the end she had to file a petition for divorce with the magistrates.

23.7 While Agis the king [of Sparta] was away on campaign, Alcibiades seduced his wife Timaea. She fell pregnant and never denied who was the father. When the boy was born she called him Leotychides in public. But in private whispers to friends and servants, the mother called the boy 'Alcibiades'.

39.5 Alcibiades caused his own death. He seduced a girl from a well-known family, and had her move in with him. The brothers of this girl were outraged by the insolence of the insult and one night they set fire to his house. When he rushed out, they killed him.

6TH HOUR OF THE DAY
(11.00–12.00)

THE
CAVALRYMAN
REVIEWS HIS TROOP

The cavalry commander studies the ten young horsemen before him, trying to project a certainty that he does not actually feel. These youths are far from competent cavalrymen, and there's not much time to prepare them. He now rather regrets that he asked for this. A month ago, he suggested to the military finance committee that it was time for Athens to raise another troop of cavalry.

The cavalry is highly regarded in Athens. During the recent war, while the Spartans were ravaging the fields of Attica, the Athenian militia was kept behind the formidable walls of Athens itself. (The regular army was away fighting in Thrace.) This saved them from being slaughtered by the deadly hoplites of Sparta, but it had been hard to watch from the walls while farms and orchards burned.

But almost every morning of the siege the cavalry had sallied out to do what they could in hit-and-run skirmishes and ambushes that amounted to guerrilla war on horseback.

This was possible because, while the Spartans are the best infantrymen in the known world, their cavalry is mediocre at best. The Athenian horse is easily a match for Spartan cavalry, even without its allies – horse archers from Scythia and Thessalian horsemen. (Thessaly produces the best cavalry in Greece, which is why Athenian cavalrymen often include Thessalian gear in their outfits.)

This is a new unit, raised to replace losses through age, disease and other attrition. (Such as poverty – though state subsidies help with a cavalryman's expenses, he is expected to bear most of the cost. Food and stabling for the minimum of two horses is pricey, and the cost of a groom needs to be added.)

Apart from two hundred horse archers, there are a thousand cavalrymen in Athens. They are commanded by two *hipparchi*, each of whom has five *phylai* under him. Subordinate to these are the ten *phylarchi* – the cavalry commander being one such – who each commands a squadron of ten men.

As the law requires, once he had obtained permission from the boule, the commander had recruited the men for his *phylum* (squadron) from those best qualified by wealth and bodily fitness. By and large he got his recruits through persuasion rather than outright conscription. In fact, most of those exempted from service by the courts had appealed for exemption at the commander's urging. Better that an impartial court finds a man unfit, lest there be suspicion that he was bribed to excuse someone from service.

The new cavalrymen are young, so their parents and guardians needed persuading. 'Look, your son has the potential to be a brilliant horseman. You pay for cavalry horses anyway through taxes, so why not have your son ride them? And once your son has a state horse, he won't buy expensive horses for himself. Furthermore, you no longer need a riding instructor, because that's my job.'

The Hippeis (Knights)

The Athenian cavalry was a social class as well as a military unit. That class regarded the Athenian democracy with deep suspicion and many yearned for the 'good old days' when aristocrats were in charge and the peasants knew their place.

The knights got their chance after the final defeat of Athens in the Peloponnesian War when the city's Spartan conquerors set up an oligarchy. This turned into a tyrannical despotism. So unpopular did the knights become that in 404 BC they were overthrown in a popular revolution, and the esteem with which the cavalry had formerly been held comprehensively disappeared.

So by flattery and diplomatic arm-twisting, the commander got his squadron together. Now, he needs to get these beginners into shape for the big parade. The public expect a show from their cavalry when there's a festival. At the Great Dionysia parade the cavalry commander will show the trouble and expense to which he has gone in raising his troop as it performs alongside the rest of the Athenian horse. His reward is recognition and approval from his fellow citizens.

The young riders have formed an untidy line in front of him. On the left, young Callicrates' legs are far too rigid – if he bumps something braced like that, he'll fracture a bone. Mysthenes is holding his reins too high and too tight – if the horse ducks its head unexpectedly he'll get pulled off. Meanwhile, Xenophon sits on his horse as though on a chair. All very well for a civilian, but a cavalryman needs to brace himself with his thighs. That way he can strike with a sword or hurl a javelin without falling off. The commander does his best to stifle a sigh.

He points to the statues of the Herms. 'Men – that's the starting point of the Dionysian gala ride right there.' (Herms are a sort of pillar with a bust of Hermes at the top. The rest of the pillar is smooth stone, except at groin height where the Herm sprouts a phallus with a formidable erection. Sometimes those leaving from a festival hang garlands there. There is room for plenty of garlands, because these Herms form a double line between the Painted and Royal Stoas.)

'Now, while the theatrical choruses are doing their ritual dance at the Altar of the Twelve Gods, we will mount and ride around the Agora offering homage to the various shrines and statues.

'When the circuit is completed, we gallop at top speed to the Eleusium.' He indicates a flat stretch of ground that finishes at the western foot of the Acropolis. 'We go in companies, in batches of a hundred. Just as in battle, there will be veteran units in front of you and behind, so you just have to keep your station. Then we split into two columns of five hundred for the parade to the Lyceum.

'We won't worry about those parts – it's all fairly straightforward so long as you remember to keep your body well back in the gallop. Right now, we'll practise the spring mount. Then down to the gymnasium to practise javelin-throwing. Mounting and throwing javelins are when you are most likely to fall off and embarrass me and yourselves.

'Dismount! Prepare for inspection!'

The commander does not expect to find much wrong with the kit itself – these are, after all, the sons of some of the richest men in Athens, and they'll have the best gear available. There's no uniformity, because there is no standard cavalry uniform. Six out of the ten wear Boeotian helmets, which pleases the commander. These helmets are a metal variation of a popular cloth hat, and as such provide protection from both sun and missiles. They give all-round vision (important for a cavalryman who does much of his work in the open) and allow the wearer to easily hear shouted orders.

The remainder wear Phrygian helmets. There's some variety here, because no two of these helmets are exactly the same. The general idea is that the high, outward-sloping sides should deflect downward blows on to the wearer's heavily padded shoulders. Those shoulders are mostly covered with a *linothorax*. The commander likes these because they are lightweight and flexible. As the name suggests, a *linothorax* is a linen cuirass, arranged in layers and stiffened with glue. Compared to a bronze cuirass, it's also cooler – and that's an important consideration. A cavalryman spends very little time actually fighting, but an awful lot of time riding under the sweltering Greek sun.

Almost everyone has a *kopis*, which makes sense. After all, the fathers of these recruits were cavalrymen themselves and know what weapons work best. The exception is young Apollodatus, who wears the shorter *xiphos* sword. The commander draws his own machete-style *kopis* as a demonstration, and gently advises the young recruit, 'Change that *xiphos*. When on horseback you want a slasher rather than a stabbing sword.'

He whisks a backhand cut through the air by way of demonstration, and the recruits lean back. All are uncomfortably aware that over the coming years they will encounter such blades more intimately, and at least two or three of them will perish in the process.

The young men are in the age group called *ephebes*. A few months ago, at the Temple of Artemis, they jointly swore a solemn oath. They would never abandon their arms or comrades, they would defend Athens until their last breath, and they would strive to leave the city a better place before they died. Now they are beginning their training for war, because warfare is a regular part of the life of every able-bodied Greek male.

Being at the early stage of their training, these eighteen-year-olds will miss the forthcoming Athenian expedition to Sicily. Instead (doubtless to the relief of their mothers) the troop will join the garrison of towns or forts in Attica, there to receive further instruction by watching and emulating veteran cavalrymen who are reaching retirement age. After two years in the ephebiate, the youths officially become men, and assume the full responsibilities and privileges of Athenian citizens.

At present the raw recruits are proud, nervous and rather embarrassed by the scrutiny of passers-by in the Agora.

'Ignore them,' says the commander. 'But remember that they are there. As cavalry, you are the pride of Athens. Work to deserve that.

'Xenophon – mount up.'

A young cavalryman, whose lower face is a battleground

between a nascent beard and pimples (the pimples are currently winning), reaches for his horse's bridle. The horse snorts and steps aside until Xenophon reaches under his armour and fishes out a carrot.

'Good,' the instructor approves. 'You need to give him a reason for wanting you on his back. A treat is one such reason. Well, go on, mount up. Don't go looking for a mounting block, use your spear for a spring mount.'

That spear is beside Xenophon, impaled into the dirt by the small secondary spearhead set in the butt. Called a *xyston*, the spear is almost twice Xenophon's height. It's the cavalryman's primary weapon, serving as a javelin, lance or thrusting spear. There's one further role, and that's the one it will serve here – vaulting pole.

'The spring mount, gentlemen, has saved more cavalry lives than I can count. You've all seen it. Stand back from the horse, so, take three steps and …' As he runs forward, the commander seizes his spear near the top, and twists as he throws out one leg. He lands on his steed with a thump, and with a deft flick of his wrist frees the *xyston* from the ground so that the lance ends up pointed between the horse's ears.

The spring mount is how a cavalryman goes from pedestrian to fully prepared fighting machine in less than five seconds. If, for example, a squadron of Corinthian horsemen suddenly appears on the ridge above a cavalry camp, you want everyone mounted and good to counter-charge in seconds flat. Otherwise enemy horsemen hit while everyone is running around looking for a mounting block or someone to give them a leg up.

Also, since Greek horses don't have stirrups, it's not that uncommon to get unhorsed in combat. A well-trained warhorse will wait around for its rider to get back on, but if

ATHENIAN HORSEMEN ON THE PARTHENON FRIEZE

that rider can't do it from a running jump, the chances are that he won't live long enough to do it at all.

Young Xenophon knows all this. He has practised often enough in the corral at his father's farm. But it's another thing to do it here, in the Agora with his new squad and half the world looking on. He carefully shifts the strap of his sword-belt, takes three quick steps, stabs down his spear and vaults. The spearpoint hits a stone just below ground level and skids. Xenophon gets two feet in the air and comes down in an untidy mass of arms, legs and weapons. The rest of the squad look on, trying desperately to keep straight faces.

It helps that the commander is very matter-of-fact about it all. 'That's the problem with unfamiliar ground. At a stable, you know where the soft ground is. Here, you find it the hard way. Well, help him up, someone. Stab the spear in first. Then run up to it, grab high, and swing yourself on to the horse. Anyone else want to try? Okay, Mysthenes, you're up.'

Xenophon

No one is certain of the exact birth date of Xenophon, but he was certainly a teenager in 416 BC. His father was wealthy and a member of the cavalry, which makes it reasonably certain that Xenophon's first days as a cavalryman were as described here.

Xenophon became famous when he was recruited as a mercenary by a Persian usurper to overthrow the Persian king. The attempt failed, leaving Xenophon and 10,000 other Greeks stranded deep in what is now Iraq. The Greek leaders were invited to peace talks and treacherously slain, which left Xenophon in command by default. The Greeks struggled through hostile terrain to the shores of the Black Sea in an epic journey known today as the 'March of the Ten Thousand'.

Xenophon wrote of this, and much else besides, when he was exiled from Athens and became a guest of the Spartans (whom he hugely admired). Xenophon's history of Sparta after the Peloponnesian War survives in a far-from-unbiased text called the *Hellenica*.

Mysthenes is a broad-shouldered, confident youth who needs no second urging. Three steps and he has swung himself into the air above where his horse used to be.

That horse, having rolled back an eye to watch events, has declined to be a part of them. The steed neatly sidesteps and Mysthenes comes down hard on his back, helmet hitting the ground with a thud. This draws cheers and applause from spectators who have realized there is free entertainment on offer.

The commander glares at the crowd and resumes his instruction. 'Pay attention to how your horse reacts when he is about to receive a rider. Many horses will baulk at something if they know beforehand that hard work will follow. You have to train your horse to stand for mounting. Otherwise, when it comes to the crunch, a disobedient horse is like a traitor. Xenophon, you'll be my model. We'll go through it slowly.

'First, until you are sure of your horse, hold the lead-rope ready in the left hand. The other end should be fastened to the bridle's chin-strap or the nose-band. Keep it loose, like so. You don't want to jerk the horse's head when you mount, but keep it tight enough that he can't pull that side-stepping trick.

'When you have made your spring, pull yourself higher with that left hand. Throw the leg right over without bending your knee, and don't touch the horse's back. With the foot over, clench those buttocks as you come down. It will hurt otherwise. Later we will practise mounting on the off-side. You never know when you'll have to do that, too.

'Now let's break for lunch and let these idle peasants who stand around gawping find something more constructive to do with themselves.'

The Cavalry Commander and *On Horsemanship*

Most of this chapter was written twenty-four centuries ago in these two works by one of the young men we meet here – Xenophon. He wrote when he was older and wiser, but his texts doubtless incorporated much of the instruction he received as an ephebe in Athens.

The recruiting techniques, armour and weapons are Xenophon's actual descriptions. So too is the description of the parade for the Great Dionysia, laid out in even greater detail than there has been space for here.

The technique for spring mounting is again taken verbatim from Xenophon, but supplemented by wisdom from re-enactors who have taken pains to get it right.

THE COUNCILLOR
TAKES HIS
LUNCH BREAK

After a tense morning, members of the boule welcome the chance to stretch their legs, move about, and sound each other out to get a sense of how matters are proceeding. Nericius was hoping to slip away for a convivial lunch with his mistress before the afternoon discussions, but clearly this won't be the case. The councillors are taking a working lunch and Nericius will spend at least part of it with the appalling Critias.

When not being a member of the boule, Nericius cares for the extensive ranchlands of the Philaidae family on nearby Euboea. Many of that family are friendly with the very aristocratic Critias. (One of Critias' ancestors was a close friend of the great Athenian law-giver Solon, and he won't let anyone forget it.) Therefore Nericius gets to be patronized by a man into whose face he would much rather push his egg-and-lettuce salad, while he smiles and pretends to recognize the obscure literary references Critias likes to sprinkle into his speech.

'I appreciate your caution about this Sicilian expedition,' Critias remarks, settling himself on the bench next to Nericius. 'It shows that it is right for everyone to hold office, whether they get it through the lottery or are elected. But is your complaint only that it looks as though Alcibiades will lead it? He is qualified after all.'

He was on the boule and had taken the Counsellor's oath. By this he bound himself to give his opinions in accordance with the law.

XENOPHON *MEMORABILIA* I.I.18

Nericius has a mouthful of salad, and so cannot reply. Critias is really just listening to the sound of his own voice anyway. 'I mean, the common people don't usually demand to share generalships or cavalry commands. These are jobs that affect the safety of the state, so they need to be well managed. Generally you people prefer more profitable salaried positions, don't you?'

Nericius notes the phrase 'you people' and bites into his lettuce with extra vigour. He swallows, and remarks politely, 'The backbone of the city is "those people" – the rowers, the steersmen, the shipwrights and the sentries. They are the strength of the city, more than the aristocrats or even the hoplite class, so I suppose it is only right they have a share in decision-making.' Nericius himself belongs to the hoplite class, but he doesn't bother to point that out.

It helps Nericius to preserve his temper that they are

sitting outside the Tholos, a part of the administrative complex beside the Bouleuterion where the morning debates have taken place. His bench against the building's wall looks across the Agora. Nericius could have eaten inside, for there are proper dining tables in the Tholos, but a fresh breeze from the sea has cleared away the morning clouds and infused the normal city stink with the scent of salt and seaweed. The sun is bright, the air fresh, and the lively bustle of the market intrigues a man accustomed to the gentle pace of country life. Every prospect pleases and only Critias is vile.

'Well, that's what visitors find most extraordinary. That in Athens the lowest people, the poor, are the ones who get more. That's why the best people oppose democracy everywhere else on earth. With us aristocrats you get minimal extravagance and injustice, and you get maximum, scrupulous care to do the right thing. With the masses, there is a maximum of stupidity, disorder and wickedness. Poverty makes them uneducated and ignorant.'

Critias' support for the Sicilian expedition had been savagely criticized that morning, and that had evidently stung. 'So you say that we ought not to let everyone serve on the council, or be on equal terms within it?' asks Nericius as mildly as he can. He offers Critias some cheese, hoping that a full mouth will bring silence. The gambit fails. Critias is in full oratorical flow.

'Oh, it's an excellent idea to let the dregs of the people speak,' he remarks sarcastically. 'Any wretch can stand up and promote his own interests, and his supporters know they will benefit more from his crude self-serving ignorance than from a good man's virtue and wisdom. What I don't understand, Nericius, is why you – a good man, so they say – sometimes take the other side. Don't you want good government for the city?'

'Is that good government in which the common people are slaves? Because even if it's a bad government, people still prefer that because it is *their* government. I've noticed that some aristocratic altruists seem good at proposing laws that benefit themselves. And once aristocrats set policy, "madmen" like myself get excluded from the council or making speeches, and it all ends up with the subjugation of the commons.' Nericius feels proud of that delivery. 'Subjugation of the commons' is the sort of phrase people throw around at symposiums. 'What you are calling bad government is the source of the people's strength and freedom.'

Critias

Critias was a great-uncle of Plato and a friend of Socrates – a friendship which later helped to get Socrates condemned and executed.

Critias was not merely socially inept – he was dangerous. When the long-expected war with Sparta resumed in 413 BC, Athens was eventually totally defeated. The conquering Spartans set up an aristocratic government to replace the democracy. Put in charge, Critias failed utterly. During a reign of terror in which some 1,500 people were executed, his government became a byword for brutality and corruption. When rebellion overthrew his tyranny, Critias was among the first to be killed.

Critias regards him with a thoughtful and unfriendly stare, and bites into his cheese while contemplating his response. Nericius realizes that he has shown more of his true feelings than is diplomatic.

After all, he can see the point of the Sicilian expedition. Athens is not at war with Sparta or Persia, but the Spartans definitely regard the task of containing Athens as unfinished business. If Athens can add Sicily to her empire that would make the state much stronger. But while the army is in Sicily, the Spartans are right here. From the Acropolis one can see Mount Parnon – and the Spartans in their acropolis looking east can see that same mountain. That's how close the two cities are.

So the question is, can the Athenians and Spartans trust each other? The Athenians virtually tore up their peace treaty with Sparta when they fought alongside Sparta's enemies at Mantinea a few years ago. Now Athens is assembling the biggest invasion fleet Greece has ever seen. From a Spartan point of view, what's to stop that fleet from landing at Pylos and taking Messenia from them? Athens nearly did it in the last war, so why not now?

That was the issue debated in the council that morning. Critias and his pro-Spartan friends have heard from contacts in the Gerousia, the Spartan council of Elders, that they are worried that the Sicilian expedition is a pretext for an Athenian sneak attack.

'Let's join the others,' says Nericius, who sees an opportunity to close the conversation. 'We'll talk to Democritus – he's the councilman closest to Nicias. Perhaps Democritus can tell us if our senior statesman has any plans to resolve the conundrum. After all, it was Nicias who negotiated peace with the Spartans five years back.'

Critias stands and, in doing so, collides violently with the slave who has come to gather their plates. Critias staggers back, and glares at the unperturbed slave who calmly collects Nericius' plate as well as Critias' own – largely untouched – food. Critias looks indignantly at his disappearing meal.

However, the slave knows that the horn to re-start the meeting will sound soon and has instructions to collect the lunch plates so that the council can come to order in a disciplined fashion. Therefore he ignores Critias' glare and calmly walks off, leaving the councilman fuming.

Nericus knows that slave. He's Boeotian, from an estate he used to manage on the other side of the Cytherean mountains. His father and uncles were killed in the war,

HOPLITE SHIELDS WERE HIGHLY INDIVIDUALISTIC AND SAID A LOT ABOUT THE WARRIOR BEHIND THE SHIELD

he was captured, and the family are having trouble paying his ransom. The boy is taking well to city life, though. It wouldn't surprise Nericus if he stayed on in Athens after being freed.

'He should be flogged,' Critias snarls. 'The slaves and metics in Athens are out of control, the lot of them. You can't hit them, and they won't even stand aside for you. I tell you, in Athens these days, we are slaves to our slaves. In my household ...'

Which is why, generally speaking, prisoners-of-war such as the young Boeotian are not kept in private households. While an unransomed prisoner is technically a slave, if he is of the hoplite class his slavery will not be onerous. The fortunes of war make it all too possible that the captors might one day find themselves also unwillingly enjoying the hospitality of an enemy city. Therefore such prisoners are treated gently, and often set unpaid work within the city's administration.

Some lower-class prisoners are skilled craftsmen, and these might be purchased and set up with a workshop. Thereafter a slave works like any other artisan, except that once a week his owner comes by and collects a substantial chunk of his earnings. Usually, by way of extra motivation, once the craftsman has paid off a pre-arranged amount he is set free. Those buying freedom on a hire-purchase plan tend to be self-conscious about it. This makes such slaves less, not more, easy to push around than free men of the same status.

Critias complains, 'When you have a city with rich slaves, then it's no longer profitable for the slave's owner that his slave might fear you. In Sparta, my slave would fear you. But in Athens if slaves could be intimidated by free men, then any free man would extort money from rich slaves. No such problem in

Sparta, where no one has any money anyway. Here, if you are not his owner, a slave thinks he's your equal. Same with the metics. It's a flaw with the system.' (In Athens – unlike some other Greek cities, slaves can be quite wealthy. Therefore they have to be protected from extortion, robbery and assault lest the free population simply help themselves to a slave's money. Slaves are well aware that only their owners can harm them, and are consequently less subservient to others – such as the fuming Critias.)

When Nericius first came to the city he too was somewhat startled by the casual attitude of urban slaves. Country slaves are more polite. But there are slaves and then there are *slaves*. The Thracians and Illyrians on the estate he considers little better than domestic animals. Their Macedonian overseer is a different class altogether, but nowhere near an equal. On the other hand, the young Boeotian slave at the Tholos has free friends, and after working hours he hangs out with them at the tavern.

'I wouldn't call a metic equal to a slave in the metic's hearing,' says Nericius. 'The metics are a bit sensitive that way. She, or he, might prove your point about their insolence by flattening your nose.'

'And get away with it,' retorts Critias bitterly. 'In the courts they disenfranchise the aristocrats, fine them, exile or execute them. Juries nowadays exist to promote the interests of the lower class. They are not interested in justice but their own advantage.'

The pair enter the Tholos and blink at the sudden change from the bright sunlight outdoors. Several councillors take advantage of this temporary blindness to suddenly engage their neighbours in conversation, or make it plain they are in a hurry to finish eating before their plates too are whisked away. It becomes clear to Nericius why Critias stepped outside to engage him in conversation. The alternative was to stand indoors alone.

Nericius is also eager to leave Critias. 'We had better go into the chamber,' he says genially. 'Andocides is heading the meeting this afternoon, and he's very short with those arriving late.'

And along with all these offices is the one that is supreme over everything. Often the same office is in charge of carrying out the business that it has proposed, or presides over the general assembly in places where the people are supreme. The institution that convenes the sovereign assembly will naturally end up as the dominant power in the state. It is styled in some places the Preliminary Council (boule) because it proposes the business to be dealt with in Assembly meetings.

ARISTOTLE *POLITICS* 6.1322B

A new chairman of the boule is selected each day to prevent any particular faction from getting an advantage. The chairman keeps with him the keys to the treasury and the archives. Daily selection makes it harder for those planning sabotage or a coup to get their hands on those vital keys because no one knows who will have them come nightfall. Over the year, two-thirds of the councillors will have been chairman.

The afternoon meeting will be busy. Tomorrow's agenda has to be drawn up and published (people like to know what the city's executive is up to), and the committee finalizing details of the approaching Dionysia will report. Above all, financing for the planned Sicilian expedition has to be worked into shape so that the Athenian Assembly can either accept the entire proposal or send it back to the boule for re-working.

Nericius is aware that Critias doesn't care if they keep working until nightfall. Today he is one of the seventeen. The seventeen are a rotating group of councilmen who stay at the Tholos for a further eight-hour shift before being replaced for the last eight hours of the night. The chairman is on duty for the full twenty-four hours. That way, Athens always has a functioning government. Late-arriving ambassadors and messengers with urgent tidings know where to report, and if there's a fire or serious civil unrest late at night, someone is around to give orders. Should an emergency arise this evening, Nericius sincerely trusts that whatever Critias wants to do will be voted down by the other sixteen duty councillors.

Nericius hopes the meeting will finish early. Then he will hurry to the little house on the south slopes of the Colonus hill where his lady awaits with chilled wine. They'll drink it on the balcony as the sun sets and the shadow of the Hill of the Nymphs slowly creeps across the rooftops of the Melite district. The lady is a metic from the island of Chios, and will be suitably outraged when Nericius informs her that Critias considers her no better than a slave.

Then homewards through the darkening streets to Limnai and his surly little wife, Tymale, whose social skills are as poor as her cooking, her weaving and her love-making. That's the price, Nericius reflects, of being a respectable married man.

The Old Oligarch

Again, this chapter basically re-works an Athenian text. The opinions here are extracted verbatim from a contemporary rant usually called 'The Old Oligarch' (or Pseudo-Xenophon). Given Critias' known views and literary aspirations, however, it would surprise no one if he was the old oligarch himself.

There is a contrary view that the text is really pro-democratic because it contains some powerful counter-arguments. These I have put into Nericius' mouth.

THE SLAVE WOMAN IS WORRIED

Athoa accompanies Theocritus as he returns to the house. The pair have just come from the courts, where Theocritus' stepbrother Antiphon has served a petition demanding custody of Athoa and her fellow slave, Phylele.

Angrily, Theocritus tells Athoa that he instructed Antiphon to take his petition, fold it so that there were plenty of sharp edges, and shove it. Hearing this, Phylele gives a wail of relief, and Theocritus responds with a grim smile. Athoa knows that, if the situation merited it, Theocritus would torture the pair himself. But Antiphon is making a grab for the family inheritance, and Theocritus won't see his valuable slaves damaged for another's greed. Yet Athoa says nothing, for as she well knows, the danger has not yet passed.

Antiphon won't give up. It will help his case that the family have refused to surrender their slaves to him for questioning, especially as he claims they were involved in a matter as serious as the death by poisoning of an Athenian citizen.

Fourteen years ago a man called Philoneos, a friend of the mother's now-deceased husband, had stopped at the house before travelling abroad on business. Philoneos had a slave concubine called Dilitira, but he was bored with her. Before he departed from Athens, Philoneos intended to sell Dilitira to a brothel. That much everyone is agreed upon.

However, according to Antiphon, his stepmother passed on to Dilitira a message of hope. The slave woman, Phylele, would give Dilitira a vial of love potion that the mother had brewed herself. If Dilitira were to slip that philtre to Philoneos in his wine, he would immediately fall back in love with Dilitira, and she would be saved. Of course, since the husband would be sharing the wine from the same urn as Philoneos, he would be dosed also, but what wife minds her husband loving her more?

The mother shakes her head. 'She didn't get the potion from me. They – Philoneos and your father – were staying together at the Piraeus. If you remember, your father was about to travel to the island of Naxos on business, and Philoneos was going there to sacrifice anyway, so they went down to the port together.'

Everyone knows there are a dozen places in the Piraeus where you can get a love potion. Theocritus assumes that the desperate Dilitira probably asked some sorceress for the strongest dose possible. The important thing to know about most love potions is that the effects are cumulative. You add a drop to your victim's food each day and his passion slowly grows.

But Dilitira didn't have days. She was being sold the next day. So once she had the potion, from whatever source, when she served the wine after dinner she gave almost the entire dose at once to Philoneos. Then she poured what was left into the father's drink. Philoneos died on the spot. The father lasted twenty days before he died, too.

Afterwards, Dilitira claimed that she acted alone. She was tortured after the killing and she did not implicate anyone else, even when they broke her bones. So there the matter rested for fourteen years. Now, during a dispute over the family inheritance, Antiphon has made his extraordinary claim that this stepmother was the source of the poison, and the slaves her accomplices. Furthermore, he claims that 'love' was never intended, but rather that the 'love philtre' had been simple poison.

It helps the family's defence that the slaves are still here, fourteen years after the alleged poisoning. After all, a cold-blooded poisoner would have surely disposed of such inconvenient witnesses long before. The slaves are completely in the power of Theocritus' mother, the alleged poisoner.

Antiphon's deposition states that he intends to get the 'truth' out of the slaves by force. There's no possibility that someone half out of her mind with terror and pain can lie consistently, so Antiphon wants the slaves tortured so that they will reveal their part in the foul deed. Of course, if the family actually do surrender the slaves and the slaves stick to their stories, that puts the mother in the clear.

Athoa imagines the tortures and is much less certain. It was fourteen years ago. Even with a clear head and an excellent memory she can't remember something that precisely – and she knows that if it comes to that, she will indeed be half-mad with terror and pain.

And all Antiphon needs is to find something – anything – that Phylele and Athoa remember differently and he will use that as proof that they are lying, making way for further and more brutal tortures. In the end they might say whatever he wants to make the pain stop.

Athoa closes her eyes. She turns into a gibbering wreck if her owners so much as produce the whip. She can hardly imagine what she'll be like at the sight of a branding iron. She forces herself to be silent, for fear of being thrown out of the room.

The mother wasn't at the court for the deposition. As a woman she cannot represent herself – the law says that her sons have to defend her against the poisoning charge. So Theocritus now updates her. 'According to Antiphon's deposition, you confessed. While Father lay on his deathbed, you came to him and informed him that you had prepared the poison. You told him how you had taken advantage of the slave girl's desperation and tricked her into thinking your vial of poison was a love potion.

'In short, you admitted that you were the killer and that poor deceived girl was merely your agent. Oh, and you did all this gloating in front of Athoa.'

Athoa thinks back. They were indeed both there by the dying man's bedside. They tended to him and did everything the doctor said. And Antiphon – he was a boy then – came up just once, maybe twice when he thought his father was only sick. He was there all the time when he thought he might lose his inheritance.

According to Antiphon, that's when his father told him what his stepmother had confessed. Antiphon claimed before the judges that he was ordered by his dying father to bring his murderer to justice, and now he is a grown man, he is doing his solemn duty – much as it pains him to act against his own family.

After Theocritus has reported this, there is a thoughtful silence. Athoa wonders why, if the father was well enough to force such an oath from his son, he was not also well enough to order his son to bring a magistrate to witness him changing his will and disinheriting his wife. He could also have accused her on the spot. Yet oddly enough, he did none of these things.

A COURTESAN APPEARS BEFORE A TRIBUNAL

'Ah,' says Theocritus, who has been thinking on the same lines. 'But Antiphon can claim that Mother prevented him from leaving the house. He was a minor at the time, remember?'

'And the doctor?' wonders Athoa. Could the mother also prevent the doctor from coming and going? Could she keep Antiphon from talking to the doctor, and the doctor from talking to the father? Hopefully all these questions will be raised by the defence. Of course, that's why Antiphon came up with the mother's 'confession' in front of Athoa. He's desperate. If he can't torture an admission out of the slaves, he has no case, and if the mother is not condemned, he has no inheritance.

'It will come to court anyway,' says Theocritus cynically. 'Only one thing terrifies an Athenian householder more than the Spartans, and that's his own wife. You'd think there was an epidemic of husbands dropping dead around Athens, there's such an obsession with wives and poison. With the public mood as it is, the Archons will want a full public hearing.'

'And I'll be Nessus, as Philoneos is Herakles,' remarks the mother wryly. In the well-known myth Herakles was slain by his wife, who – thinking she had been given a love potion – had been tricked by a scheming centaur called Nessus into administering poison to her husband.

Theocritus shakes his head. 'No, he's not going with that. The parallel is too exact – it might suggest to the jury that is where he got the idea. Judging from what he was ranting about in his deposition, Mother, you are going to be Clytemnestra.'

'Clytemnestra?' remarks the mother. 'I could carry that off.' She strikes a dramatic pose.

Athoa calls up her limited knowledge of mythology and makes the connection. Clytemnestra was the half-sister of the beauteous Helen of Troy, but that's not what everyone remembers about her. While her husband was off fighting the Trojan War, Clytemnestra had an affair with her husband's cousin. Most Athenian males can identify with that situation. They spend a good part of the year away with the army or the fleet, leaving their wives alone, supposedly, at home. When Clytemnestra's husband finally returned, dusty from a long chariot ride, his loving wife prepared a bath and stabbed him to death while he was taking it.

Sure, apart from that illicit affair, Clytemnestra had plenty of reasons for wanting her husband dead. That husband had murdered Clytemnestra's previous husband, raped and abducted her, then sacrificed her daughter at the altar to ensure a favourable wind to Troy.[14] But that's not what Athenian men remember. Mostly they remember Clytemnestra when their wives offer to draw them a bath.

Athoa knows that if Antiphon successfully identifies his stepmother with Clytemnestra in the jury's minds, he will be halfway to getting a guilty verdict. If the jury finds the mother guilty, Antiphon gets the father's entire inheritance. The sons of his second wife – that wife being the mother – also lose their share of the inheritance if the mother is condemned as a poisoner. They'll lose the house, too.

Without the testimony of Athoa and Phylele, Antiphon has only wild and improbable accusations with nothing to support them. Doubtless he will exploit the suspicion every man harbours about his wife's fidelity. There will be appeal after appeal to the heavens for 'justice' and the pathos of a poor man lying on his deathbed, helpless to avenge himself on the gloating wife who killed him. He won't get far with a jury, so the family expect that Antiphon will try to get himself a lynch mob.

Theocritus lays out his planned defence. He will start by explaining Antiphon's motive. It's not revenge for a murder a long time ago – a murder that didn't happen anyway. It's greed in the here and now. There are gaping holes in his allegations, and the mother is so evidently innocent that Theocritus is not going to have their slaves crippled for nothing. After fourteen years it is possible that anyone can accuse anyone of anything. The evidence is long gone, and memories have faded. What the jurors use as a criterion for justice today might be the basis for their own condemnation or innocence in the future.

The brother is unconvinced. 'His appeals to emotion are so much stronger than our appeals to reason. Still, you are the older brother. I'll follow your lead.' Athoa and Phylele follow him out, but Athoa pauses outside the door to listen.

When Theocritus thinks he is alone with his mother, he

quietly tells her, 'I didn't want to say in front of the slaves, in case they do something stupid like running off. But I talked to some friends after the deposition. Our refusal to hand the slaves over is definitely hurting our case. To guarantee an acquittal we might have to give the slaves up for questioning.'

'No!' says the mother, and the ferocity in her voice evidently takes Theocritus by surprise. Athoa is much less startled. She strains to hear the son's muttered reply.

'I didn't know you were so concerned for them. We will have doctors, and the best care afterwards ...'

'You can't,' says the mother in a savage whisper. 'Your father was tougher than I thought. He lasted hours after I told him and I couldn't keep that little rat Antiphon away from him all that time. And yes, Athoa overheard me, curse her!'

The Facts of the Matter

The events in this chapter happened almost exactly as described. They are outlined in a text called *Antiphon: Against the Stepmother for Poisoning*. The date is uncertain, but it is one of fifteen surviving speeches by the Athenian orator Antiphon. Most experts put the date of this speech between 419 BC and 414 BC.

The argument is that when Antiphon became a successful orator, he finally became confident enough to reveal his family's guilty secret. Or, alternatively, he became embroiled in an argument with his stepbrothers about the family inheritance, and cooked up a false charge against his stepmother.

Regrettably, we do not have the stepmother's defence. Nor

do we know what the jury decided. In the trial Antiphon did indeed lead with the refusal of the defendants to present their slaves for questioning. Otherwise his case is all unfounded allegations and bluster. No impartial jury would find against the stepmother on the basis of the charges he presents. Sadly, Athenian juries were sometimes far from impartial.

THE RUNNER SETS OUT FOR SPARTA

I t is a little-known fact that in a long-distance race, a human in good physical condition can outrun a horse. The horse has a lot more weight to move along, and is propelled by grass and grain – neither of which is a particularly high-powered food. Furthermore, horses are intelligent animals and object to being forced to run at high speed over very long distances.

Labras is a runner, one of the elite long-distance messengers called *hemerodromoi* who regard horses as wimpish quitters. Like many of the best couriers, he is in his early forties. His face is very tanned and weathered, and his blue eyes have deep wrinkles from squinting at distant horizons.

The longest foot race at the Olympic games is the *dolichos*, a mere stroll of 24 *stades* (2.63 miles). Labras considers that race child's play. For a quick sprint to one of the *demes* of Attica, or to get an urgent message to Thebes in Boeotia, by all means get a young man in his twenties. But the long haul to Sparta requires a mature runner – someone with the physical and mental reserves to handle the gruelling runs that leave a twenty-year-old weeping at the roadside. Some 'long distances' are much longer than others, and it takes decades to make a proper long-distance runner.

Anyone doing the Sparta run can't help but think of Pheidippides. Around seventy years ago (in 490 BC), Pheidippides made the same run that Labras is currently embarked upon. Then, there was an urgent crisis – the Persian army had landed at Marathon intent on destroying Athens. Pheidippides was sent to ask for Spartan help. According to the historian Herodotus, Pheidippides arrived in Sparta 'the day after he set out'.

THE MESSENGER OF VICTORY AT MARATHON

Let's put that in context. Assuming that he started at the Bouleuterion in Athens and finished outside the Gerousia in Sparta, Pheidippides had to run 1,400 *stades* (245 km, 152 miles) in under forty hours. And he did that in the month of Metageitnion (August/September), when it is so hot that even mad dogs think twice about going out in the midday sun. Labras is grateful that he's doing his run in milder spring weather, though in consequence it will get brutally cold as he approaches the high passes of Tegea.

The Spartathlon

In 1982, a Royal Air Force officer intrigued by the heroic run of Pheidippides decided to check if it was really possible for a runner to leave Athens and be in Sparta the following day. Since no one seemed to know, he did the run himself, completing the 245 km (152 miles) in thirty-eight hours. Since then the Spartathlon has become the gold standard for elite long-distance runners. Of the several hundred runners who attempt the gruelling course, few make it past Corinth. No modern runner has attempted the return run on the following day.

The messages that Labras carries are verbal, although he has also a brief instruction marked with the official seal of Athens, which basically tells the sceptical listener to 'Believe this man'. The message is in a small pack which Labras has fitted to his back with such exactness that he seldom remembers it is there, unless he has need of the dried meat or honeyed figs that the pack also contains.

There is also a water-flask, though this is smaller than one might expect. Like all runners, Labras has an encyclopaedic knowledge of the springs located along his route and knows to within a few minutes how far he is from a fresh draught of cooling water. There's also a small vial of oil. Even with a loose tunic, the long-distance runner who does not lubricate his nipples will arrive with a huge bloodstain across his chest.

This is the easy part of the trip, when the muscles ease into their rhythm and Labras feels the pure joy of running. That simple act exfoliates away the tedium and petty annoyances of everyday life. Indeed, running as much as he does, friends confirm he goes 'a bit funny' if deprived of strenuous exercise for more than a few days. At present Labras is loping westward along the Sacred Way, with the groves of the Academy visible at his right shoulder and the little river Cephissus (first drink stop) not very far ahead.

At this point he is barefoot, feet slapping on the hard, dusty earth of the road in a regular rhythm. The leathery soles of his feet get the same tender affection that a cavalryman gives his horse or a hoplite his panoply. His feet are the tools of his trade, and he takes care to keep the skin smooth and oiled. Abrasions or cracks have a way of widening into bloody splits by the end of a long run.

The Sacred Way will take him east up the long ridge of Mount Aegaleos, and as he tops the ridge he will see – as do the worshippers who walk the Sacred Way every year in celebration of the Elysian rites – the late afternoon sun glinting off the waves of the Eleusian Gulf, and the white temple nestled between the sea and the Plain of Thria.

As he does every time he runs this route, Labras reminds

himself that he must take up the long-standing offer of a colleague to be enrolled as an initiate in the rites celebrated at that temple of Eleusis. What those rites are, only initiates know, for they are sworn to secrecy after their participation in the mystery. Furthermore, the Athenian state enforces this secrecy with the death penalty for those who talk. The rite is certainly ancient – by some accounts the ceremony has been held every year for the past millennium.

The theme is death and rebirth – that much is commonly known. Demeter is involved and so is her daughter Persephone. In taverns the uninitiated speculate. Hades, dread king of the Underworld, abducted Persephone to be his bride. In anger and grief for her lost daughter, Demeter, Goddess of the Corn and all crops, refused to let anything grow upon the Earth.

Lest they become gods of barren and empty desert, the Olympians prevailed on Hades to release his kidnapped bride. However, because Persephone ate three pomegranate seeds while in the kingdom of Hades, she is compelled to return there every year. So every year Demeter goes on strike and nothing grows until Persephone makes her annual return from the Underworld. As she returns, the rains fall and the land breaks exuberantly into bloom.

Perhaps Persephone returns from the Underworld at Eleusis, and is there welcomed by the goddess Demeter, while awestruck hierophants look on. But such speculation is only whispered, lest the authorities dispatch those speculating to the Underworld where they can check for themselves.

Labras ponders this as he runs effortlessly along the Sacred Way. That's the other thing about running six back-to-back marathons at once: the steady rhythm induces a sort of trance-like state. There's time to think of this and that, not in the

Raped into your marriage bed as the seasons die
You alone are life and death to mortals in our troubles.
Persephone, font of nourishment and bringer of death.

Hear, blessed Goddess and let the earth be fruitful
Blooming in healthful peace under your gentle touch
By life abundant make rich our old age
Before we enter your realm, Persephone,
The kingdom of mighty Hades.

Orphic Hymn to Persephone

usual way of things – with hurried thoughts squeezed in before the next interruption – but with steady, languid contemplation. There's nothing else for the mind to do but endure, and it helps greatly if a runner thinks of anything except the impossible demands he is making of his body.

Before the river Cephissus, Labras is still in the outskirts of the city itself. Farms cluster beside the road, with dogs – Labras would like to slaughter the entire species – running out to bark as he passes by. There's barley in the fields, and thick groves of olive trees, their leaves khaki with dust. Many of the trees are young, and some of the old trees have dark scorch marks running up the gnarled bark of their trunks.

That was the Spartans. As they discovered in the recent war, it is difficult to destroy an olive grove. Cutting the tree down works for a few years before a new tree bounces up from the roots. Grubbing the roots from the ground is hard, demoralizing work – especially if you are a Spartiate who usually leaves manual labour to menials. As for burning the trees – well, that clearly failed as those scorch marks are on trees that will soon be laden with fruit.

Still, Labras has run through this same country in earlier years, when the farmhouses were rubble and the fields empty of cattle. He knows at first hand the devastation and grief that Sparta's incursions can cause the people of Attica. Athens is the urban heart of the state, but most Athenians do not live in the city. They live in the *demes*, the little townships of Attica. Every day they leave their cottages and work the fields, men and women alike, tending fruit trees, ploughing the land and minding the livestock before coming home to participate in the age-old rituals of village life.

That is how Labras grew up, and why he intends to present the Athenian case to the Spartan Gerousia as passionately as he can. Yes, Athens has assembled a mighty fleet. Yes, their hoplite army is as large and as powerful as it has ever been. But this mighty weapon of destruction is not aimed at the Peloponnese. The chairman of the boule wants to assure the Gerousia that this comes from Nicias himself, the architect of the peace that ended the previous war, and a man who has always dealt honestly with Sparta.

Labras shifts across the road to avoid a laden ox-cart heading towards the city, and wonders again why he has been charged with this message. Surely the Athenians could put some fat, pampered ambassador on a boat and sail him at his ease across the Saronic Gulf down to the port of Gythium. From there it is a morning's walk to Sparta proper, where the ambassador could present his case without anyone breaking a sweat.

It does not occur to Labras that he, speaking with conviction, might carry more weight than any ambassador. The somewhat rustic Spartans are highly suspicious of what they regard as the

The generals sent a herald to Sparta. This was Pheidippides, a long-distance runner by profession. ... When Pheidippides was in the mountains above Tegea, he encountered the god Pan, who said he bore goodwill towards the Athenians, and had often helped them ... Pheidippides reached Sparta on the day after leaving Athens. He came before the magistrates, and addressed them.

HERODOTUS *HISTORIES* 6.105FF

slick and overly sophisticated Athenians. (Not that the Spartans can't do sophisticated, they just don't like to be obvious about it.) While disregarding a politician, they are likely to be impressed by a stringy, middle-aged athlete capable of greater physical feats than even the average Spartiate can manage.

The river is coming up, and Labras mentally marks off the first of several dozen waypoints along his run. No one can run to Sparta, because the enormity of the challenge crushes the imagination before the journey even starts. However, a run to the river Cephissus is a pleasant afternoon's outing. From there it's not far to the temple of Aphrodite at the high pass that leads down to Eleusis. Then, as night falls, there are two sections – the easy run across the plain (two watering stops) and the hills going up to the fortress town of Oenoe. Just like that, you're out of Attica and slicing Boeotia into sections before you get to your first major rest stop – Corinth – in the small hours of the morning.

Corinth is time to check the stars because the isthmus represents one-third of the journey. Ideally, Labras likes to have built up a small buffer at this point. If time allows, he will empty his bowels at the roadside, take a long, slow drink and perform tortuous exercises to ease cramped muscles. Ahead lies the tough part – the high pass at the bottom of the isthmus before the plains and the ancient city of Tegea. All in biting cold that saps the energy from an already near-drained body.

It was at this point that the famous Pheidippides saw the great god Pan urging him to greater efforts. Labras is not surprised. Long-distance runners exercise themselves to a point where the walls of reality become thin. He fondly recalls the time – on this same run – when a troop of centaurs emerged from the woods and trotted alongside him for part of the journey. Labras is still unsure whether this actually happened, but very much looks forward to it happening again.

Nearing Tegea he will have the morning sun on his left shoulder. That the road will then run downhill is less helpful than it seems. Downhill puts extra strain on his joints, and by now inevitable damage is taking place within his body. His metabolism breaks down his muscles for energy, and poisons accumulated from overwork take too long to flush from his system. Like most runners, Labras has his own theories of how best to combat this. For him it's fresh fruit – lots of it. Before a long run he practically lives on fresh fruit and lean meat.

Past Tegea, the noon sun blazes down, and with disorientation comes deep dissatisfaction with making a living by pounding through the heat on leaden legs while wondering how many toenails he will lose this time around. Labras has been there before, and while not looking forward to feeling this profound angst, it does mean that he's hit rock bottom. Physically and mentally, this is as bad as he is going to get. And there's only the equivalent of two complete marathons to go.

Hermes [the messenger of Zeus]: *I have only just got back from Sidon, where he [father Zeus] sent me to see after Europa. Before I can even catch my breath I have to rush off to Argos, in quest of Danae. 'Oh,' says father, 'and you can stop in at Boeotia to see Antiope while you are at it'. I tell you, it's killing me.*

Maia [mother of Hermes]: *Now now, my child. Be a good boy and do as your father says. Run along to Argos and Boeotia. And get a move on – unless you want a whipping.*

LUCIAN *DIVINE DIALOGUES* 4(24)

Labras will arrive in Sparta late in the evening and let the Euphors know that he has arrived. Then, in quarters assigned for messengers like himself, he'll sleep like the dead until mid-morning when he will be summoned to the council. Afterwards he will return to his room and sleep until the following dawn. Then he will be up with the sun, ready for the really difficult part – the run back to Athens.

10TH HOUR OF THE DAY
(15.00–16.00)

THE HOPLITE BECOMES INDIGNANT

Strolling towards the harbour gate, the hoplite idly contemplates the city walls. Somewhere over there, up by the ramparts, is his great-grandfather's tomb. It's a contemporary pastime in Athens, to wander the city walls and locate parts of the family property jammed into them.

The current walls surrounding Athens were built in a hurry. It all started at Thermopylae. To hear the Spartans tell it, Thermopylae (480 BC) was a great victory. In fact, it wasn't. It was where King Leonidas and his Spartans were crushed by the overwhelming force of the invading Persian army. The Spartans were valiant and defiant, but they were crushed nonetheless. (The Persians had to go through the Spartans instead of ferrying their army around them because Greek warships blocked their path. That – mainly Athenian – fleet did at sea what Leonidas failed to do on land. Few remember that now. Poets prefer pointless but heroic deaths to businesslike battles fought and won.)

After Thermopylae, the Persians descended on Athens with vindictive fury and flattened the city, taking perverse pleasure in completely destroying its protective walls. Without walls, a Greek city is as helpless as a snail outside its shell. Therefore, Athens shuddered collectively when, after the Persians had been thrown back, the Spartans said, 'Athens does not need walls. Our protection is enough. Friends look after friends. And we are friends, are we not? We would be very upset, otherwise.'

The hoplite now looking at the present walls was not even born when they were raised. His father was a boy at the time, and even at his tender age was pressed into the wall-building project. Themistocles, the Athenian leader, told the Athenians to throw up a wall as fast as they could, while he went to Sparta to assure the Spartans that the Athenians were doing nothing of the sort.

All available stonework was used by the desperate Athenians. There was plenty of rubble, because the retreating Persians demolished whatever they could not burn or loot. But even standing houses were dismantled, carried to the walls and fitted into the rapidly rising stonework. It's why the Athenian city walls are a mess. You can see a column here, part of a frieze there, and everywhere lumps of stone rudely shaped with chisels for a rudimentary fit.

Meanwhile, everyone travelling to the Peloponnese was politely detained in Athens. Of course, rumours got through. Isolated in the Eurotas valley Sparta might be, but word of such a large and controversial Athenian building project was bound to get through eventually. Themistocles, encamped in Sparta, denied every rumour. Then, as reports kept coming in, he announced he would send a delegation to find the truth.

That delegation failed to return to Sparta, while the Athenian walls kept rising. When the citizen-builders ran out of suitable stone they stripped the tombs outside the city, which is how the hoplite's great-grandfather ended up in the ramparts. By then, Themistocles confessed that Athens did indeed have walls. Large, solid and very defensible walls. What did the Spartans intend to do about it?

The walls were a rushed job, but they worked. When, inevitably, the anti-Persian alliance fell apart and Sparta and Athens were later at loggerheads, the Spartans marched right up to those walls of Athens, but they had not a chance of taking the city. That much the hoplite had seen. By then he had been an ephebe, proudly standing in armour alongside his father.

Today he has sentry duty. With Athens at peace the only danger the hoplite faces is of falling asleep through boredom. He is pleased that today he won't be patrolling the city walls, with their irregular steps and treacherously sloping surfaces; instead, he will pace at ease alongside the Long Walls to start his shift at a station overlooking the harbour.

The Long Walls are everything that the city walls are not. When the Athenians came to build them their city was flush with cash from the silver mines at Laurion and contributions from their unwilling allies. The walls are built on solid limestone foundations with custom-carved stone. It's actually easier to take the walkway along the ramparts than to walk between the walls to the Piraeus.

The Long Walls are a set of two walls running in parallel, 500 paces apart, and effectively insulate Athens from the surrounding countryside to make the city an island. Invaders might wreak havoc on the countryside of Attica, but so long as the navy of Athens is supreme, supplies will land at the Piraeus and be protected between the Long Walls on their journey to the city. Besiegers can only watch, while the occasional guard on the Athenian ramparts insultingly lifts his tunic to flash his buttocks at them.

MAP OF
THE LONG WALLS

ATHENS

Northern Long Wall

Long Wall

Southern

Phaleric Wall

PHALERUM

Phaleric Bay

Phaleric Bay

CAPE COLIAS

PEIRAEUS

Kilometers

Miles

JOINED BY THE LONG WALLS, THE VERY DIFFERENT CITIES OF ATHENS AND PIRAEUS

A flight of stone steps leads to the ramparts near the harbour gate, and the young hoplite is about to ascend these when a jovial call stops him in his tracks. An elderly man sits under the awning of a street tavern. The hoplite immediately recognizes him as one of the city's most famous sons, the playwright Sophocles.

Sophocles says to the friends who sit with him around the table, 'It's one of the city's heroes – the hoplites who keep us safe.' He waves the young man over. The hoplite hesitates, but this is Sophocles. He can hardly say no.

This is the man who led the city's *paean* – the choral chant to the gods – in gratitude for the victory at Salamis over the Persians. This was a friend of Pericles, and a drinking buddy of the general Cimon. During the Samos campaign twenty-five years previously, Sophocles was a general himself. The man is famous and powerful, and has famous and powerful friends. Unless the hoplite wants to clean latrines for the next month, he had better be polite. He comes over.

'Take a seat, my boy. Take a seat,' says Sophocles genially.

'I, um, must be on duty soon,' says the hoplite nervously. He perches next to the playwright on the edge of the bench.

One of Sophocles' hangers-on pours wine from a clay jug, splashes in some water to fill it to the brim and passes it to the hoplite, who reluctantly shakes his head.

'He can't drink that – he's going on duty,' says Sophocles reprovingly. 'I'll take it. Careful, it's full. Pass it slowly – like a *hetaira* to her lover on the next couch.' He is referring to a woman who blurs the distinction between a courtesan and a high-class prostitute.

'Now you've made him blush,' says one of Sophocles' companions. 'How did the poet Phrynichus put it? "Shines his crimson cheek like the light of love". Beautiful.'

Sophocles

Sophocles was born in 496 BC in the *deme* of Colonus, soon after the battle of Marathon. He died ninety years later, at the end of the Peloponnesian War. For most of that time, Sophocles was an active playwright who composed some 123 dramas, the last of which – his award-winning *Oedipus at Colonus* – was written the year he died, sixty-two years after he won his first dramatic award in 468.

With his Theban plays, and above all with his dramas featuring Oedipus, Sophocles took Athenian theatre to new heights, and his seven surviving plays are still regularly staged all around the world.

'Yes, you are learned in poetry,' says Sophocles, 'but Phrynichus was wrong to call a beautiful boy's cheeks crimson. If the painter smeared this boy's cheeks with crimson, he would no longer seem beautiful. It's quite wrong to compare beauty with what is not beautiful.'

The discomfited hoplite is well aware of the cruelty underlying the cheerfully inebriated badinage. He is also angrily aware that he is now blushing all the more furiously. He intends to pass the cup to Sophocles and be gone, and to Hades with good manners.

'Oh, you've got a fleck of straw in there,' says the poet to the hoplite, gesturing at the wine cup. 'Do please take it out. You want me to enjoy my wine, don't you? No!' Sophocles winces. 'Not with your finger. We don't know where it's been. The cup is full enough. Just blow it out.'

The hoplite lifts the cup and purses his lips to blow. As

he does so, Sophocles leans in closer. Suddenly he whips his arm around the youth and pulls him in for a long, intimate kiss. Stunned, the hoplite sits still in his seat, while the others burst into whoops and shouts of applause. For some reason, all the hoplite can think about as this goes on is setting the wine beaker on the table without spilling the contents. As he does this, the poet's tongue pushes past his lips. With a struggle, the hoplite pulls free, and leaps to his feet.

'You managed that perfectly!' one of the companions tells Sophocles, who preens with self-satisfaction.

'I am practising strategy, gentlemen. Pericles said that I knew how to make poetry, but not how to be a strategist. Well, this stratagem fell out just right for me, didn't it?'

Sophocles was a general with Pericles on a certain naval expedition. When he praised the beauty of one of the young men, Pericles told him: 'Sophocles, a general does not only keep his hands clean but his eyes as well.'

PLUTARCH *LIFE OF PERICLES* 8

They ignore the hoplite, who turns his back and walks off, trembling with helpless anger and humiliation. A single sarcastic farewell follows him up the steps to the ramparts.

Shortly after, when the watch commander does his inspection, the hoplite makes a formal complaint. But the commander is dismissive. Everyone knows what Sophocles is like and the hoplite should have expected as much when he sat at the table and shared a beaker of wine with him. And there's nothing he can do about it now anyway. He wasn't on duty yet, so Sophocles wasn't interfering with the watch. The hoplite could ask his father to complain on his behalf, if he doesn't mind making enemies unnecessarily, but it's not worth it. He knows he needs to forget the whole thing. It was just a bit of horseplay, after all.

Sophocles the Lecher

The incident with the wine beaker is recorded in the *Deipnosophists* of Athenaeus (13.81). In the text, the event has been moved from a dinner party in Chios to a tavern in Athens, and the youthful hoplite has replaced a young man called Hermesileus. Otherwise the incident happened as recorded, right down to the dialogue.

The guard sharing watch duty with the hoplite is equally philosophical. 'That Sophocles is a pervert, and no mistake. Men are attracted to boys around the age of puberty. That's natural. But to look for an *eromenos* – a boy love – in an adult man is unnatural. If he wasn't Sophocles, someone would have done something by now.

'Hey, did you hear about Sophocles and that thing with Euripides? Shows that there's no fool like an old fool.'

The hoplite lives a rather sheltered life with his parents. Not wanting to appear totally naive and out-of-touch he says cautiously, 'Go on.'

The guard begins his story. A while back Sophocles was outside the walls when he met a farm boy. The boy was evidently fairly used to accommodating well-off older men and they quickly reached an agreement. This ended with the two naked on the ground on the boy's cloak, with the cloak of Sophocles protecting whatever modesty the pair had left. Afterwards, the boy stood up and walked off with Sophocles' cloak.

It was an expensive cloak, and all Sophocles got out of it was the boy's smelly old thing of cheap Euboean wool. The old man made the mistake of complaining publicly about the theft – everyone laughed at him about it. Euripides made a joke of it – a quick verse about losing only a few pleasurable moments, but not his cloak. Sophocles hit back with one about Euripides' affair with a Thracian merchant's wife.

Closing his eyes, the guard recites:

I was stripped naked by the heat of the sun, not by a boy.
Unlike you, Euripides, kissing someone else's wife

...

Those who plant their seed in another's field
Are unwise to accuse Eros of snatch–and–run.[15]

'Look, after our shift, let's hit that tavern – the one over there by the docks. The owner doesn't mind if we park our kit behind the counter and have a beaker or two of wine on the way home. I'll introduce you to Athena – despite her name she's none too wise, but she is very sociable. She also lacks a grey beard, because she's fifty years younger than your last romantic acquaintance. What do you say?'

Greek Homosexuality

In a literal sense, homosexuality did not exist in ancient Athens. The word itself is actually less than 200 years old. The ancient Athenians had a completely different outlook on the matter, and took the attitude that sex was sex. By and large, as long as a man took a 'man's role', he was a normal macho male, whether the recipient of his affections was a male slave, a teenage boy, a prostitute or his wife.

That same lust for teenage boys which today would lead to a long jail sentence was encouraged in Athenian society. An older male would take an interest in his young lover's development, give him little gifts, and mentor him until he became a mature, bearded male. Thereafter the erotic part of the relationship was meant to stop, though the couple might remain firm friends for the rest of their lives.

A mature male who was on the receiving end of male affections was mocked as what Aristophanes refers to as a *euryproktos* – a 'wide-arse'. Such men were considered pathetic. Literally. The passive partner in an Athenian sexual relationship was the *patheticos*.

THE SEA CAPTAIN
MAKES HARBOUR

'There's Cantharos,' remarks one of the sailors with considerable satisfaction.

Palionautos greets the news with relief and regards the water in the ship's bilge well with a clinical eye. The morning's deep-sea swells have abated and the *Neriad* is now running northwest under sail. The old girl is not good with heavy seas. Every time the ship heaves herself to the crest of a wave or slams into a trough, the whole vessel creaks alarmingly and seawater spurts between the salt-warped timbers, making a mockery of the pitch painstakingly caulked into the joints that winter. Still, the bilge water level won't get much deeper in the quiet waters of the harbour, and pumping the ship dry will keep the sailors out of mischief while the old ship is docked.

Palionautos eases his aching joints away from the bilge pump and clambers up the mast-step on to the deck to view the approaching harbour. He wonders how long he and the *Neriad* can keep doing this. Both are much too old. Man and ship should now be sailing leisurely around the Euxine Sea (the Black Sea), taking passengers and short-term cargoes along the coast, returning every few days to his home port of Nymphaion bearing trinkets and gifts for his grandchildren. As he has done every year for the past decade, Palionautos swears that this grain run will be the last.

It's just that the Athens trip is so very profitable. The Athenians need imported grain, and offer plentiful incentives for merchants to supply it. For a start – provided that the *Neriad* manages to stay afloat – it's almost risk-free. While still at Nymphaion on the northern shores of the Euxine Sea, Palionautos agreed a price for the grain with an agent working for the Athenian *sitones*, the state's official grain buyer. Then, to buy the grain, he arranged with the agent a loan at 15 per cent interest using his ship as security.

Next, he haggled with the local wholesalers who collect grain from farmers in the interior. The objective was 300 amphorae of grain (around 6,200 litres) to be sold for at least 85 per cent profit in Athens. Since the sale price has already been agreed with the Athenian grain agent, Palionautos set sail knowing exactly how much he will make on his cargo.

There's a 10 per cent levy extracted by the authorities at Chalcedon when the ship exits the Euxine Sea, harbour dues to be paid in Athens, and the salary for the ship's three crewmen, but these costs and more will be paid by the profits from the cargo on the return trip. So the grain run is guaranteed free money. The loan is covered by the Athenian state, so even if the *Neriad* sinks on the way to Athens, the debt is wiped out.

There's another reason for the voyage to Athens – a reason that the unsentimental Palionautos won't admit even to himself. Sure, even with a good wind the *Neriad* moves slowly – but what's the hurry? All the more time to savour the feeling of perfect freedom as the ship runs between the pale blue spring sky and the deep, clear blue waters off Chios, when there is nothing to do but lie on deck watching the puffy white clouds slip by. Or the hours spent fishing off the side of the boat in a sheltered cove, seeing the shadow of the *Neriad*'s hull, dark and sharp on the white sand through 3 metres of transparently clear water.

Palionautos complains bitterly about the hardships of his job to anyone who will listen, but the simple truth is he loves being a sailor. Especially at times like this, running free and clear towards Cantharos on the Piraeus, the long afternoon shadows from the hills of Akte hiding the stoa and Emporium on the east side of the harbour, while in the distance the crooked witch's hat of Mount Lycabettus gleams in the sunshine. It's a feeling that only sailors know. Once again Poseidon has stayed his hand and guided the ship into haven, away from the sudden storms that lash the Euxine waters, the ship-killing currents of the waters below Mount Athos, and the sleek and murderous pirate vessels that haunt the Cyclades.

In heartfelt tones, Palionautos informs the crew, 'We've done it again, lads.'

Now to manoeuvre the *Neriad* to dock. The entrance to the harbour seems to stay the same distance away, though the wake curling behind the ship shows that they are making good speed. Then suddenly the column to the right of the harbour entrance – which sailors call 'the column of Themistocles' – is almost alongside, and it's time to trim sail and for Palionautos himself to take the twin oars at the back of their ship, which serve as the rudders.

The *Neriad* is the type of ship merchantmen called the *kerkouros* – a 'trimmed tail' – for a *kerkouros* is almost flat-backed. When she gets to the docks, the *Neriad* will moor stern-first, bows pointing into the harbour. With the back of the ship secured to bollards, and a gang-plank down the middle, unloading will be a straightforward process.

While his ship is docked, Palionautos has to decide something he has pondered through the voyage. Basically, the matter is this: the *Neriad* is ancient. The pine of the ship's wooden hull was cut from the hillsides around Aleppo when Palionautos was a boy. He's sixty years old now, and the ship is not much younger. The mast step has twice had to be moved up to accommodate a larger bilge pump, and even so, every voyage is a race against the rising water in the hold.

The ship was originally built in the traditional manner – first the planks of the hull were carefully fitted together, and then, when the shell of the ship had already been constructed, the ribs were inserted within and secured with copper spikes. Palionautos remembers when his father had purchased the ship, mortgaging the freehold on the family smallholding to do so. She had been a lively little boat that positively skipped over the waves, delighting the boy who had once hung on to the rigging lines, laughing up at the brightly patterned sail.

The *Neriad*

The *Neriad* is actually a ship called the *Kyrenia*, a shipwreck found off the coast of Cyprus during the 1960s. Like the *Neriad*, this ship was elderly – around eighty years old. Even then the *Kyrenia* did not die naturally. Spearheads embedded in the hull suggest the ship was taken by pirates, who afterwards scuttled it as not worth saving. So intact were the ship's remains that a new version was reconstructed. Named the *Kyrenia II*, this ship still plies the waters as an ambassador of Cypriot culture.

For more about this extraordinary vessel see the *National Geographic Society Research Reports* (vol. 13) of 1981.

That sail has now been replaced several times, and even the latest version is patched and faded. Still, the sail is the least of Palionautos' worries. The problem is the hull. Palionautos is too veteran a mariner to think that his luck can last.

Once day a vicious gale will howl down from the mountains of Euboea. Tall, choppy waves will swirl the ship around like a wood chip in a barrel. If the frail old ship is not simply torn apart by the currents, she'll take on so much water that she'll founder. Even on this relatively peaceful voyage, heavy seas opened gaps of almost a finger's breadth in the hull, spurting water into the hold. Palionautos glances sourly at those gaps, now roughly caulked with oil-soaked cloth.

So should Palionautos accept that the *Neriad* has made her last Aegean run? Is it now time to finally retire the old ship for her final years as a decrepit coaster? Or should he blow the profits of this and several past voyages on a refit to keep the *Neriad* afloat for another decade?

Athens produces abundant silver. But the galena ore mined at Laurion is an amalgam of lead and silver, so extracting the silver means separating out the lead. Therefore lead is cheap in Athens. What Palionautos is considering is a remedy often used to keep old ships afloat – a skin of beaten lead, sheathing and waterproofing the hull.

The *Neriad* is 26 cubits (12 metres) from bow to cut-off stern, and 9 cubits (4.3 metres) at her widest. So even with relatively cheap lead, this will be an expensive operation. Also, there is a trade-off. A thin layer of lead will flex with the ship, and eventually split, leading to further leaks. A thicker layer will provide better protection, but the weight will lower the freeboard, so the ship carries less cargo. The need for ballast, however, will also be cut. Palionautos mulls it over and decides that he'll talk to the chandlers at the

Choma, the jetty. At least he should get some estimates for the work. Then—

'Ship! 'Ware ship!' calls one of the deckhands, startling Palionautos from his reverie. A big Phoenician trader is bearing down on them, intent on beating the *Neriad* to the harbour mouth. These ships carry 300 tons of cargo packed into almost 30 metres of length, and their captains are infamously intolerant of smaller shipping in their way. Indeed, with over a dozen sailors on board, not only can these ships fight off most pirates, but they are also sometimes pirates themselves should they catch an unwary smaller ship at a lonely anchorage.

The Phoenician is high in the water, making Palionautos suspect that the cargo is papyrus from Egypt, perhaps supplemented with sandalwood and spices from India. The merchantman is making twice the speed of the *Neriad*. Palionautos must lean hard into a steering oar to pull his ship aside. Angrily, he orders the crewmen to spill wind from the sail to keep them from running aground on the breakwater. Palionautos notes the stylized bull emblem on the Phoenician's prow. He will register a vehement complaint with the harbourmaster's officials when they come aboard to collect their 1 per cent docking dues.

The *Neriad* has lost her momentum so the deckhands have to unship the long oars that will scull them to their berth. A crewman studies the harbour walls.

'Where's Thrasyllos? He usually sits there – just above the chains.' (In wartime, these chains are locked across the harbour mouth at night – a reminder of the time when a daring Spartan commander had once planned a naval commando raid right into the heart of the Piraeus.)

'Thrasyllos? He's gone,' says Palionautos absent-mindedly. His attention is on steering, which is harder now the *Neriad*

THE PORT OF PIRAEUS, WITH ATHENS IN THE DISTANCE

is not properly underway. 'You weren't here last time, or you'd have heard.'

Thrasyllos is a harbour legend. An amiable lunatic, Thrasyllos believed that all the shipping in the harbour was his. He would perch on the harbour wall and record the comings and goings of 'his' vessel in a meticulously kept log book.[16]

'What happened?'

'His brother. He got tired of Thrasyllos' craziness and took him to a doctor. The doctor knew his stuff, and he effected a complete cure.'

The crewman curses. 'That's no good. I liked the old man. He would let me look through his logs, and see if any of my friends were in port. At least if their ships had docked recently, I'd know they were well. Thrasyllos was practically a public service. It's a pity he was cured.'

'Thrasyllos felt the same,' remarks Palionautos. 'He was never happier than when sitting in the sunshine watching "his" ships. He tried it again after he was cured, but it didn't work. He runs cattle on the family estate near Aexone now.'

The *Neriad* glides into harbour as the sun sinks towards the horizon, and Palionautos feels quiet satisfaction at having arrived in perfect time. They have travelled the entire day, and had they arrived two hours later, they'd have had to either moor offshore, or run the ship on to the beach at nearby Phalerum because it would be too dark to get properly docked in crowded Cantharos.

The old sailor scans the quays. Cantharos is one of three harbours on the Akte peninsula. To the east is Zea harbour, once the grain harbour of Athens (hence the name – *zea* is the word for emmer wheat). Now that harbour is a base for the ferocious Athenian war fleet, but the grain warehouses are still situated nearby, uphill from the Emporium, so that's the side where Palionautos will dock.

A harbour 'lighter' ship laden with produce crosses the *Neriad*'s bows, a cage of chickens reminding Palionautos that on the morrow he must sacrifice to Hermes and Poseidon for his safe voyage. As the boat moves from their path, Palionautos points.

'Over there – that's our berth.'

12TH HOUR OF THE DAY
(17.00–18.00)

THE CITY PLANNER IS CROSS-EXAMINED

As the twilight deepens outside, Phanagora lights the first in a row of little oil lamps at the back of the tavern. She's starting a new amphora of wine and wants to make sure that the sediment in the urn has properly settled. Yesterday, a patron had pointedly asked for his wine to be poured into the Spartan campaign cup that he had brought along for the purpose. These cups have a series of concentric rings indented into the inside. This is all the better to trap debris if the cup is dipped into a muddy stream, or alternatively to catch the lees from a poorly filtered amphora of wine. Phanagora prides herself on the quality of the fare she serves, so the implied insult had stung. Now she carefully checks the product, even though this particular amphora is 'black wine' from Chios and almost opaque.[17]

The early evening crowd are rolling in – workmen dusty from their labours, shopkeepers from the Agora, and artisans from the many small manufactories scattered around the Piraeus. Some are slaves, some are metics and some are native Athenians. Phanagora does not really care so long as their coin is good. There's also a smattering of travellers from the docks. Many like to stop here for a quick bout of refreshment before taking the long stroll between the Long Walls up to Athens proper.

One such traveller seems to be the long-haired foreigner sitting in the corner, twirling an oiled lock of grey hair around his forefinger as he gazes disapprovingly down the street. His tunic is cheap lambswool, albeit warm and comfortable, yet the rings on his fingers are Italian-worked gold. Phanagora is a bit uneasy about that. Most of her patrons are a good crowd, but there's always the odd bad apple who might be tempted into a bit of street thievery if the victim is evidently a foreigner.

'Those stalls, down there – who permits them?' he demands of Phanagora when she comes to top up his wine. 'They are permanent structures and should be removed. The whole point of that street is that it should carry away water in a heavy rain.'

A TERRACOTTA OIL LAMP. ONES FROM PRIVATE HOUSES WERE OFTEN MUCH MORE ELABORATE

'It's not really a problem,' remarks Pentarkes, who has come downstairs to help his mother-in-law with the evening shift. 'The street is on an incline, and the rainwater just washes around them.'

'Not the point,' insists the stranger loudly. 'We're next to Munchyia here, and under that hill everything is so hollowed out and undermined – partly by humans, partly by nature – that you can fit whole houses into some of those tunnels. If the street is not properly drained here, then the water back flows to the Munchyia and causes problems there.' He jabs a finger at the offending stalls. 'Those things should not be there.'

'You seem to know a lot about local geography for a foreigner,' remarks one of the tavern regulars.

'Of course I do,' says the stranger. 'Munchyia – hill and harbour, that way. Main road to Akte and the grain warehouses, two blocks that way. Quickest way to the main harbour, three blocks that way, turn right. And when you get there, tell the authorities that the piping from the fountain at the intersection could use some repair. Can't the collective Athenian intellect get its head around the concept of urban maintenance?'

The workmen look a bit defensive. As far as they are concerned the Piraeus works fine. It has straight streets, arranged so that the wind blows the stink and smoke away. Also, the streets are nicely angled so that the houses catch the sun. For twisty old streets, decrepit houses and a water supply so old no one knows where the pipes are, one has to go to the *asty* (the city of Athens proper). The people of the Piraeus like it where they are.

A workman looks at the stranger suspiciously. 'Who are you, anyway?'

'I am Hippodamus!' The stranger spreads his arms wide, and performs a sort of sitting bow, like an actor receiving applause in the theatre. The revelation is greeted with thoughtful silence.

Hippodamus. The name is certainly familiar. The local agora south of the new theatre is the Hippodamean Agora. The name also pops up on a few other local structures and an intersection near the harbour. This is because Hippodamus was responsible for the design of the whole Piraeus.

After a long pause a voice from the back says, '*That* Hippodamus. I thought you were dead. Ages ago.'

'Not dead,' retorts the city planner. 'Living in Thurium in Italy. Though now you mention it, that's almost the same thing.'

Phanagora, meanwhile, is staring through the tavern windows, down the darkening street. When she was a girl, that view was just rubble and goat tracks. She recalls that Pericles himself hired Hippodamus to make a proper port town of it all.

Hippodamus once claimed that this was because Pericles had been deeply impressed by his work in the rebuilding of Miletus after the Persians had destroyed it in the Ionian Wars. Pericles liked the idea of streets laid out on a grid plan, and he asked Hippodamus if it was possible for the same thing to be done with the Piraeus. It was Hippodamus' fond claim that until he did it first, no one had ever thought of making straight streets that cross the others at right angles.

Yet, despite this boast, Anatolia was packed with cities with a grid layout, and those streets had been there for over a thousand years. Even Miletus, according to those with long memories, had been put back together into very much the same shape as it had been before the Persians took it apart – grid pattern and all.

'Anyway, rebuilding Miletus was a long time ago. You couldn't have been more than a teenager when the rebuilding started,' Phanagora says.

'I'm older than I look,' retorts Hippodamus. 'There's not much alternative to clean living in Thurium. If I didn't do my grid in Miletus, why else would Pericles have hired me?'

From a seat near the wine casks, a full-bearded man with long wavy hair raises his hand like a schoolchild. Dropping easily into the role of teacher, Phanagora points an authoritative finger. 'Antisthenes, pupil of Socrates. Stand and answer.'

'Because you wrote *Elements of City Planning*. Pericles was really impressed with it. And your idea of dividing city land into public, private and sacred, and then conceiving of a city as a single mechanism with integrated parts – Socrates says it's revolutionary.'

Antisthenes knows the topic well. Socrates has rather a lot to say about Hippodamus, and Antisthenes has tactfully chosen the more polite bit. Socrates also thinks that Hippodamus' theories on social engineering are, in his words, 'the kind of deranged fantasy you get from a know-it-all who tries to talk about politics when he has no practical experience.' That critique was specifically about Hippodamus' proposed division of the city's people into three classes – artisans, farmers and soldiers. 'What's to stop the soldiers simply taking over the state?' Socrates had demanded. Antisthenes is about to put this point to Hippodamus when Phanagora forestalls him.

'Thank you, Antisthenes. You may sit down,' she says. Now she turns to face Hippodamus. 'Our Socrates has offered you a compliment, albeit at second hand. How do you respond?'[18]

'By demanding more wine,' says Hippodamus. 'If I'm to go on about urban design for the entertainment of the gentlemen here, I deserve to drink at your expense. It's only fair.'

Hippodamus was the son of Euryphon, a Milesian. It was he who cut up Piraeus with his invention of cities divided into blocks. He developed a somewhat eccentric lifestyle. Some people thought him a dandy, because he liked to stand out with his expensive jewellery and flowing locks of hair. Yet he wore cheap but warm clothes whatever the season. He wanted to be thought to be a man of wide learning in the sciences and was the first man who attempted to speak on the subject of the best form of constitution without having any practical knowledge of the subject.

ARISTOTLE *POLITICS* 2.1267B18

His drink refreshed, Hippodamus launches into an exposition he has evidently recited dozens of times before. 'First thing, don't assume your city is complete. It's a living entity, like a tree. It's going to grow and change. You have to allow for that. So when you plan, be flexible. The basic unit for building a house is the brick. The basic unit for building a city is the city block, created by roads running north to south and east to west.

'Now, you aim to have your important structures in the middle, spaced apart to avoid traffic congestion, and with the main roads running alongside them, not through. Compare the mess that is the Agora in Athens with my creation, the Hippodamean Agora. Instead of having not one but two thoroughfares running right through it, my Agora has the road running alongside it, straight to the temple of Artemis. And that road is sixty cubits wide to accommodate festival crowds, processions or whatever else you want to stage there.'[19]

Hippodamus refrains from mentioning that Pericles didn't completely trust the unruly populace down at the port, packed as it is with metics, traders and foreign influences. So, he had Hippodamus make the main road broad, straight and clear. This is wonderful for traffic, but the real reason for the wide street is that its very breadth makes it harder for rioters or rebels to build a decent barricade across it. In fact, the street is wide enough to allow a unit of hoplites to proceed in good formation right down to the harbour.

This last bit of information would undoubtedly upset the unruly elements, foreigners and metics who make up Hippodamus' audience. Aware that some cynical individual might make the same point at any moment, Hippodamus hurries on to explain the logic behind favouring straight streets.

Pericles wanted the Piraeus as a model city. When water travels along a gutter on a street with too many twists and turns it overflows, and dirty run-off water interferes with the delivery of clean water to the houses. Hippodamus argues that if the blasted authorities would maintain the pipes properly, the water supply in the Piraeus is vastly superior to that in the *asty*. That's because the streets run in straight lines, so you can lay pipes right down them.

Phanagora nods in silent agreement. She lives in a Hippodamean house. When her family moved in, the Athenians were building ten houses a week in the Piraeus – sometimes twenty. All have the same plan: two storeys, a small garden and a kitchen at the back. Because everyone knows where the bedrooms and entrances are, it's easier to fight fires and deliver water right to her door. She has to admit it – the Piraeus works as a place to live. Whatever Hippodamus' defects as a person, as a city designer he certainly knows his craft.

'So what tempted you away from Thurium?' asks one of the audience, diplomatically topping up Hippodamus' wine cup by pouring out his own. 'Was it a desire to return to Athens and critique your own work?'

'Rhodes,' replies the city planner. 'I'm on my way to Rhodes. It's going to be a great city one day, mark my words.'

This gets Hippodamus some puzzled looks. The more well-travelled members of the audience know that Rhodes is not a city at all. It's an island with a collection of villages sprawling higgledy-piggledy all over the hillsides.

'I've been commissioned to survey the island and pick out a site for a city,' Hippodamus continues smugly. 'Just as the ancient Athenian king, Theseus, united the *demes* of Attica and made Athens the capital, the villages of Rhodes are amalgamating into one city. And I'm going to design it for them. Despite all my imitators, the people of Rhodes still want the original and best.'

'Imitators?' asks Phanagora incautiously. The response is vehement.

'Yes! Imitators. I call them thieves. It's a better name for them. You steal the purse from a man's belt, and you are justly punished as a thief. Yet they steal the ideas from a man's head – ideas that are far more valuable – and they are lauded and rewarded for the theft. If there were any justice in this world, every time someone laid out a grid plan for a township a payment would be due to me, Hippodamus, who thought of it first.' He pauses, recalling the critics' mention of the ancient grid plans in Asia Minor.

'Apart from barbarians. What they thought of doesn't matter. We don't owe them anything. But the state should reward those who come up with ideas that are of benefit to the city, just as they reward the sculptors and painters who beautify it and the soldiers who defend it. Yet not only are my ideas given for free, thereafter they are stolen by others.'

Antisthenes piles in yet again. 'Yet when your purse is taken by another, you have no purse. When your ideas are taken by another, do you not still have those ideas also? It's as when I light my household fire from your hearth. I take the flame, but you have it yet.'

'I can see why you are a student of Socrates,' snarls Hippodamus.

'Also, the danger of rewarding the man who comes up with bright ideas is that we create a market for ideas. This is Athens. We've all the bright ideas we can handle. Yet what if a man decided he could do better by keeping silent and then selling his ideas to Thebes, or Corinth?'

Rewarding anyone who discovers something useful to the state is an idea which sounds good, but it would make dangerous law. It would encourage informers, and perhaps even lead to political disturbances.

ARISTOTLE *POLITICS* 2.1268

There is a mutter of agreement from those present. Some are turning back to their drinks, others ordering supper from Pentarkes. Private conversations are starting up around the room. Hippodamus has clearly lost his audience. The city planner gets to his feet with exaggerated dignity.

'I see I am wasting my time here. There are places in the city where I will be welcome and appreciated. I have tarried here too long. Terrible wine, by the way.' Hippodamus throws a few obols on to the table in front of Phanagora, and stalks out into the gathering twilight.

Assessments of Antisthenes
(later a prominent philosopher of the Cynic school)

He lived in the Piraeus, and every day would march five miles to Athens in order to hear Socrates.

...

Being a metic, he despised the Athenians for their airs, saying, 'So what if they are sprung from their native soil? So are snails and wingless locusts.'

Diogenes Laërtius Book 6 passim

More intelligent than educated.

Cicero (to Atticus 12.36)

An absolute dog.

Plato (from Diogenes Laërtius 6.2)

THE HETAIRA
PREPARES

Thargelia carefully wrestles a calfskin slipper on to her dainty foot. 'I like the sound of this Autolycus character,' she remarks. 'Even if he's not intellectual enough for this symposium.'

Aspasia regards her young protégée carefully. Thargelia knows that one reason Aspasia likes her is because she was herself mentored by an older *hetaira* of that same name. Apart from anything else, Aspasia learned a lot from the original Thargelia's mistakes. The older Thargelia married fourteen times in all, which is the Athenian matrimonial record. Aspasia herself has been married twice.

There was Lysicles the wool-trader, killed in Caria while collecting taxes from recalcitrant Athenian subjects. Before that was Pericles, leader of Athens until the plague killed him during the war with the Spartans. Actually, 'married' is a bit strong, because as an Athenian from one of the city's top families, Pericles could not marry a foreigner (Aspasia originally hails from Miletus).

Nevertheless, Pericles found Aspasia sufficiently friendly and welcoming (which is what the name 'Aspasia' means) that he divorced his previous wife and lived with Aspasia in unmarried bliss. While Pericles was running Athens, many suspected that the hidden hand of Aspasia was running Pericles. Even now it is believed that Aspasia controls the city more than the current Archons.

Milesian Aspasia, model of wisdom. Admired by the admirable 'Olympian' [Pericles]. Political knowledge and insight, shrewdness and perspicacity [were hers].

LUCIAN *PORTRAIT STUDIES* 27

Cratinus calls her 'a prostitute past shaming'.

PLUTARCH *LIFE OF PERICLES* 24

This would not surprise young Thargelia, who will provide companionship to top Athenian philosophers and politicians at a symposium tonight. She was hand-picked for the job by Aspasia, and carefully briefed on the personalities and quirks of all present. Tomorrow she will report in detail who said what to whom, which friendships seem strong and which social alliances are fraying.

'Don't worry about Autolycus,' Aspasia brusquely informs her protégée.

Thargelia's target for tonight is to be Nicoratus, the son

of Nicias. Nicias and Alcibiades are currently the two top politicians in Athens. Aspasia keeps close tabs on Alcibiades through her friendship with Socrates. This is easy enough, as Alcibiades regards Socrates as a sort of father-confessor. Discovering what Nicias is thinking is harder. The old politician is both shrewd and suspicious. But suitably prompted, his drunk and randy son might provide some insights. That's why Thargelia has the task of keeping company with him tonight.

'But Autolycus sounds divine. Can't I have him instead?' complains Thargelia.

'No. Concentrate on Nicoratus.'

It's true that Autolycus may be something of an oaf. He gets lost in a sentence with more than one minor clause, and his idea of wit is pouring wine on someone's crotch. For all his physical charms, Thargelia concedes that she would be wasted on him. Anyway, it would annoy Callias. He's hosting this event ostensibly to honour Autolycus' success in the Olympic pentathlon. But really Callias wants Autolycus for himself, and he won't appreciate competition.

Aspasia passes a garment from the rack. She has obviously chosen that *peplos* with care. It is yellow, with high slits up the thigh and cut nicely to show off Thargelia's bust without being obvious about it. A symposium girl should dress attractively, but look neat, not cheap.

Be subtle, Aspasia has warned. Nicoratus should think he is the chooser, not the chosen. He likes clever women, but clever in a good way. She can't talk too much, and should keep looking at her victim until he gets the hint. She is to nibble daintily at food, instead of stuffing her cheeks like a packrat.

There is to be no making fun of playwrights this time – though Thargelia believes she would have plenty of material were she so inclined. (Her problem with playwrights came at a recent symposium where Thargelia had poured a kylix of wine for the playwright Aristarchus. When Aristarchus remarked that the wine was well chilled, the smiling girl replied, 'Oh, I dipped it in one of your love scenes.' Amusing perhaps, but Thargelia's lack of self-restraint had permanently lost her a well-paying lover.[20])

Callias will need Autolycus amenable if he's to get his way, so expect unwatered wine. Aspasia tells Thargelia to sip – not gulp. Even being tipsy takes you off your game, and a drunk woman at a symposium is not appreciated.[21]

Thargelia has taken all Aspasia's advice without resentment. She'll suffer criticism all day as the price for getting personally coached by Aspasia. Athenian wits say that Aspasia is a better teacher than Socrates. Aspasia trained Pericles, while the prize pupil of Socrates is the abominable Critias.[22]

'How are things with Messenaon?' enquires Aspasia while Thargelia gets dressed.

The courtesan pauses with a brooch half-clasped at the shoulder. She suspects that Aspasia well knows how things go with her on-again, off-again lover, but is making conversation to pass the time.

'Well, if a *hetaira*'s house could be maintained on tears, I'd be doing well. Every time I say I'm leaving him I get tears in abundance. But this job takes money, clothes and jewellery. Would it be too much to have a maidservant take care of my basic needs? I don't have a family estate at Myrrhinus, the Attic village where the wretched Messenaon owns property, and I don't own a share in a silver mine. My life runs on offerings from my halfwit admirers.'

All she receives from Messenaon is a set of earrings, a necklace and a tunic from Tarentum that she is embarrassed

A HARPIST AND HER MIDDLE-AGED ADMIRER

to be seen in. She believes that if she demanded a serious present from him, he would accuse her of plotting to set fire to the dockyards or some other serious breach of the laws, just to get shot of her.[23]

A stable of lovers is one of the things that differentiates a *hetaira* from a prostitute. Athenian women can't be *hetairas* because the men feel this thins the pool of available wives, but there's no stigma in the profession itself. Even the common prostitute (*porne*) is despised not for taking money for sex – which the Athenians regard as a perfectly legitimate transaction – but for having a regular employer in her pimp or madame.

In Athens, a regular job with a single employer makes one barely a step above a slave. A slave looks to one man for food, housing and clothing. It is hardly different when one man instead supplies the money with which food, housing and clothing are purchased. Ideally, a free man lives on his resources – investments or family property. Failing that, he or she leverages skills or physical attributes in the marketplace. Socrates receives gifts from students in return for intellectual stimulation. No one thinks less of Thargelia because she supplies stimulation of a more physical nature.

Once, when a moralistic individual criticized a *hetaira* for ruining the morals of young men, she coolly replied, 'Does it matter whether they are corrupted by a *hetaira*, a politician or a philosopher?' Young men like female company (most young men – those inclined towards their own gender find plenty of takers among their elders) and, since an aristocratic Athenian male marries only in his thirties, until then his choices are prostitutes, *hetairas* or celibacy.

And even older, married men like to keep company with *hetairas*. They are an important component of Athenian social life. As both Messenaon and Thargelia are well aware, however, there's a tension between the *hetaira* and her lovers. On the one side, as in any free market, there's the danger of competition. If his company and gifts don't measure up, or someone better makes her schedule too crowded, a *hetaira* will ditch a man without a second's hesitation.

The *hetaira*'s ideal beau is young, good-looking, lavishly and unfailingly generous, intelligent and good-tempered. Sadly the species has been hunted to extinction, so *hetairas* compete viciously for any man with just two of the above qualities. They know that if they are not constantly charming and interesting, then these men will desert them for someone who is. The free market is not slavery, but no one claims it is nice either.

Thargelia puts on the *peplos* and poses prettily for Aspasia. Having received her mentor's approval, she sits and begins to apply makeup. Aspasia steps behind her to dress her hair. Persian girls are dark, so Greek girls like to sport blonde hair. Left to itself, Thargelia's hair is naturally a sort of muddy brown – but it has not been left to itself for quite a while. Thargelia regularly soaks her tresses in vinegar to bleach them, then exposes her hair to the noon sun to draw out the colour. This is tricky, because the sun also makes hair dry and brittle, and no proper courtesan has anything but porcelain-pale skin. Thargelia gets around this with olive oil shampoos and shading her face under a broad-brimmed hat with the top cut off.

Now she dips a little brush into a pot containing a mix of honey, olive oil and charcoal, and starts to add eye shadow. Not too much, because she will whiten her face with lead powder and wants to look alluring. Some girls end up with faces looking like skulls.

'How does Nicoratus like eyebrows?' she enquires, never doubting that Aspasia will know.

'Separate,' comes the crisp reply. Thargelia is pleased. She dislikes the fashion for monobrows, where girls not naturally so blessed use cosmetics to join their eyebrows to a single line above their noses. She bites into a cloth saturated with red pigment to stain her lips, and then critically examines the result in a hand mirror. (This type of hand mirror with its typical cross-guard has since become the symbol for 'female', just as the hoplite's shield and spear symbolize 'male'.)[24]

Thargelia is wondering why Aspasia has not chosen to use

one of her own girls tonight. Of course, Aspasia would deny that she has any girls. Yet it's an open secret in Athens that, through proxies, Aspasia runs one of the best brothels in town. Aristophanes once announced this publicly in a play where 'two harlots were kidnapped from Aspasia's bawdy house'.[25]

Thargelia fishes for an answer, 'I mean I'm flattered that you trust me.'

Aspasia never pauses in braiding Thargelia's hair. 'You remind me of me when I was younger, my dear. Not just pretty, but intelligent and enterprising. A girl who plans for the future, to have an income even when her lovers and her looks are gone.'

Thargelia stiffens with shock. She tells herself, Aspasia doesn't know. She can't know. Thargelia has been so careful.

Aspasia cheerfully continues to prepare Thargelia for the evening. Reaching into an open box she selects some bangles which she fits to the girl's wrist. As she does so, she continues in light, gossipy tones.

She tells Thargelia of a new sorceress, operating from the Scambonidae district. 'Very effective, they tell me, though of course I don't believe rumours. It's what a *hetaira* might do, even if she had some time free in the mornings. Perhaps she takes discreet lessons from that woman who lives out by Keremeikos.' The woman is supposed to be a witch, though no one has ever proven anything.

At the mention of Keremeikos, Thargelia's hand has jerked violently, sending a smear of makeup across her cheek. Aspasia tuts as she helps to repair the damage. If she notices that Thargelia's hand is trembling slightly, her mentor gives no sign of it. She continues chattily.

'Taking lessons from that *magissa* is no bad idea, though I would think she depends too much on mind-altering pharmaceuticals and neglects good old-fashioned people-management. And she overcharges for henbane. You can get it yourself, you know, in the pastures out by Ceriadae. There's a farmer there called Aelion. Tell him I sent you.

'But don't use the henbane for sorcery. That would be bad, very bad. There are so many laws against it.'

Both women know that if the identity of the Scambonidae sorceress is revealed, those many laws demand the woman should be arrested, tortured and painfully executed.

Gloomily, Thargelia realizes why Aspasia has chosen her for the job of fishing for delicate information at the symposium, and why she will probably be carrying out similar tasks in the future. Aspasia needs someone whom she can trust with her life. And from now on, Thargelia's life is in Aspasia's hands.

Aspasia

The widow of Pericles was a remarkable woman. As a non-Athenian she was free from the domestic servitude to which Athenian men sentenced their wives. She was involved in public life, through her husbands and on her own account. She was also suspected of playing a larger role behind the scenes.

How Aspasia ended up in Athens is uncertain, though later classical writers gave her the 'kidnapped from Miletus, enslaved in Caria, captured and sold in Athens' backstory that has here been passed to the slave-girl character of Chryseis in 'The slaves get playful'. Regrettably, all the information we have about Aspasia comes from sources biased one way or another.

'So! It's just as well neither of us is into sorcery,' exclaims Aspasia brightly. 'Now you were asking why I trust you with the job of fishing at the symposium for such delicate information? Instinct. I took one look at you and thought, "I like this girl. I feel I could trust her with *her* life." Are you ready to go?'

2ND HOUR OF THE NIGHT
(19.00–20.00)

THE FIG-SMUGGLER
ARRANGES A
SHIPMENT

Gerochus the farmer enters the tavern and glances around to see if he recognizes anyone. It's hard to tell, because Phanagora keeps the lighting to a few oil lamps near the wine amphorae. She even dislikes having the lamps at the windows, though this is necessary to let customers know that the establishment is open. She does this, not from parsimony, though olive oil is expensive, but mainly because naked flames, olive oil and drunks do not play well together in a confined and flammable space.

So the room is a shadowy place, with the drinkers mere dark silhouettes hunched over their cups, squinting at dice or engaging in the passionate, high-volume conversation-arguments that are an Athenian speciality. Gerochus has chosen the place and the hour so as to be anonymous. The person he is meeting is there – the grey man in the corner with his back to the room. He is accompanied by a large and truculent sailor who glares at anyone who even thinks of taking the stool opposite.

But as Gerochus slips past and pulls up the stool the sailor merely nods and wanders off in search of refreshment. Gerochus had collected a drink from the landlady as he went by, and now takes a swig, paying no attention to the man opposite.

Evidently the *Neriad* made good time getting into harbour. Which, admittedly, is more than Gerochus has done getting to the tavern. Palionautos had expected this meeting to happen over an hour ago.

However, Gerochus had to get back from his orchard. And he prefers it when the tavern is gloomy so people won't recognize him. All it takes is someone who also knows that Palionautos is a sailor and they'll be exposed: fig farmer plus sailor clearly signals a smuggling operation. If the authorities suspect Gerochus of illegal activity, things could become difficult for all of them.

Gerochus knows that Palionautos thinks these precautions over-dramatic. After all, the old sailor lives across two seas and does not fraternize with Athenians. Yet still he might be recognized by harbour officials or other sailors. Actually, all it would take to trip them up would be a tavern patron observant enough to see that Gerochus is talking to someone with a deep-water tan. No – better the business gets done after dark. The Athenians have zero sense of humour when it comes to people exporting their beloved figs.

Palionautos is silent for a moment. Then he asks, 'How are the figs this year?'

Gerochus shrugs. It's a bit early to tell. The season's shaping up, and there has not been much rain recently. (If it rains while the fruit is ripening, the figs split.) But Gerochus' first harvest is looking good. If that goes well, then he'll have a bumper crop in late summer. 'All is well,' he replies. 'I'll always have figs for you, thanks to my little wasps.'

Gerochus refers to the unusual symbiosis between fig trees and their wasps. Every type of fig tree has a specialist wasp evolved to live and breed within just that fig. Figs are not really fruit at all, but a specialized environment called a syconium. Within the syconium, tiny fig flowers develop without ever seeing sunlight. They are fertilized by equally tiny fig wasps, which mate in one syconium before the females lay their eggs in another, thus spreading the pollen. The actual 'fruits' of a fig tree are the many tiny single-seeded fruit contained within the skin of the syconium.

The fig wasp has a short (but thanks to its environment, very sweet) life of weeks or even days. This has affected human development because, to keep their insect symbionts alive, fig trees are among the very few plants that produce some fruit all year round, with the bulk of the fruit coming in the spring and late summer. Because they produce a consistent food supply, fig trees were among the first domesticated plants. There were fig orchards thousands of years before wheat fields.

The first figs arrived in Greece from the Middle East. Indeed, the name for the trees in Gerochus' orchard, *Ficus carica*, reflects the Greek belief that the trees came from Caria in Asia Minor. But as far as Gerochus is concerned, his figs are native to Athenian soil, given to a grateful populace as the bounty of the god Dionysus. Sweet and tasty, figs are the food of Olympic champions and the restorer of health to the sick. (Which is none too surprising as figs are packed with fibre, vitamins and minerals.)

'So the usual load? One-fifth fresh, the rest dried?'

By 'fresh', Palionautos means picked the day he sails. He has got to ship his highly perishable cargo across the Aegean and straight to market in Cyzicus. One bad headwind, and a fortune goes rotten in his hold. The fresher the figs the longer they last, and even the freshest figs don't last that long – a week at best.

Fresh Attic figs are a delicacy even in Athens. They taste fantastic, but they rot quickly. And because figs stop ripening as soon they are taken off the tree, they can only be picked ripe. Thereafter it's a race to get them to market. Most figs are sold dried, which Gerochus much prefers. If pests (human, animal and insect) are kept away from the finished product, dried figs can remain in storage for up to a year. And another way that figs are different from most fruit is that figs have almost the same nutritional value dried or fresh.

Getting the dried figs on to the *Neriad* will be a simple matter. For months, Gerochus has been quietly stashing barrels away for that purpose in a hidden cellar under the orchard work shed. The fresh figs are trickier. The morning that the *Neriad* sails, Gerochus will strip his orchard of all the ripe fruit he can find. Fresh figs have to be discovered by careful examination – the ripe fruit feels slightly soft when squeezed, and sometimes the skin cracks to reveal the pulp beneath.

There will be figs enough, but only just. Once again Gerochus feels a bitter spasm of hatred towards the Spartans who hacked down his beloved trees during the last war. Those were mature trees, several times the height of a man. Some were hundreds of years old, producing their bounty for Gerochus, his father and generations before that. All killed by Spartan hoplites in a pointless spasm of destruction. The gods curse them.

It is only this year that the new trees have started to bear fruit. Gerochus, with tears streaming down his face, had selected two-year growth from the fallen trees, and carefully prepared cuttings from which his new trees would rise. Four

THE MARKET IN ANCIENT ATHENS

years, it had taken. Four years of working as a labourer by day and tending saplings by night, and only now were his trees producing fruit. Even so, Gerochus needs another eight years before his orchard is back in full production.

Palionautos will pay cash on receipt of the goods. He could not pay earlier even if he wanted to (and he doesn't want to) because he won't have the silver until the grain merchants pay him for his cargo. But at least Gerochus will get paid in Athenian coinage – pure silver minted into Attic owls.

'The war was easy enough on you merchantmen, wasn't it?' remarks Gerochus rather bitterly. 'You were safely away in the Euxine guarded by the Athenian navy – I even pulled an oar around in those parts myself. Meanwhile, my livelihood was destroyed at home while I was away protecting yours.'

'Oh, easy. That's what it was, when your navies were so busy fighting each other that no one suppressed the pirates who came swarming over the seas like flies over a dead dog. Yet when you saw a strange sail on the horizon, you hoped it was pirates. They would just ransom and ruin you, but if the Spartans or their allies found you carrying grain to Athens, they killed you on the spot. If you don't like foreigners that much, why sell me your figs – especially since it's against the law?'

It is a sore point. Gerochus is a smuggler because of the debt he accumulated while he was getting his orchard working again. He had received no help from the Athenian state. City voters vote in the interests of city folk, and the problems of country farmers don't seem to concern them much. They want fresh figs cheap, even if it bankrupts the growers, so Gerochus feels no shame in selling to the highest-paying customer. They're his figs; what right do those in the city have to keep him from selling to anyone but themselves – at rock-bottom prices, too?

Tomorrow Palionautos will go to Gerochus' home while the farmer is in his orchard. Gerochus has stashed a couple of sacks in the toolshed so that his customer can examine the goods. Then they will agree the price.

This price is determined by several factors. Firstly there's the competition. Palionautos is not the only merchantman in Athens who doesn't mind picking up a high-value cargo on the way home, even if that cargo is illegal.

However, most merchants can smuggle a sackful here, or mix a barrel in with the salted fish there – only the *Neriad* will take a full harvest, and both Gerochus and Palionautos know it. Also, with the Dionysia coming, the Agora is full of value goods. Palionautos can still do well if he takes a cargo of Italian cloaks and Sicilian cheeses home with him this time.

But Gerochus knows the sailor will certainly check his

samples, because no legitimate cargo can offer anything like the same profit margins. He is offering quality figs, because this time they're from his own orchard. He has even set up a bowl at home for Palionautos to run checks.

This has become necessary since the cargo of illicit figs Gerochus had procured for the *Neriad* two years ago. Because his own trees were not yet producing, he had begged, borrowed or stolen what he could from the farms of Attica and even harvested figs from wild trees in the rocky ravines on the Boeotian border.

The suspicious Palionautos had demanded a bowl of water. Then he selected a random fresh fig, halved it with a sailor's knife and placed the halves face down in the bowl. Gerochus had watched miserably as a small maggot quickly wriggled free. Over the next five minutes others followed, and when Palionautos removed the figs, some twenty maggots remained in the bowl, some small as grains of sand, others almost as long as his little fingernail.

Gentlemen of the Jury, many people have come to me, expressing surprise that I have come to the council to accuse these dealers. They say that, no matter how guilty they may be, those who deliver speeches against them are sycophants.

LYSIAS 22 *AGAINST THE GRAIN DEALERS* (PROLOGUE)

'A merchant on Thasos showed me that trick,' Palionautos had remarked conversationally, 'in the process of slicing my profit margin by three-quarters. Apparently the maggots look almost exactly like the white fibres within the fruit, so you don't find them until they try to escape from drowning. Did you know that? I'm sure you did.'

Picking up one of the dried figs, Palionautos had scraped away a layer of seeds with his knife. Holding the translucent skin up to the light, he demonstrated how to check dried figs. This specimen had been infested with fruit-fly worms and some larvae, as well as the occasional dead fruit beetle.

Thereafter the deal had been renegotiated, with prices going steeply downwards. On that occasion, Gerochus had settled for little more than he would have got selling the figs to unwary Athenians in the marketplace. Ever since, his quality control has been rigorous. On this occasion, the figs are from Gerochus' own orchard and he is eager to show off their quality.

Palionautos smiles. Gerochus had been deeply embarrassed by his sub-standard produce, and both parties know that this time around the figs will be excellent. Gerochus suspects that Palionautos is probably looking forward to enjoying a few himself on the voyage home.

Depending how the refit goes, one night soon the *Neriad* will quietly run up the sandy beach at Phalerum, where Gerochus waits with his illicit barrels in the dunes. Everyone will work fast, rolling the barrels down the beach on to the wet sand and manhandling them into the hold. Then they will carefully add several sack-loads of fresh figs to the smuggled cargo, and a significant amount of silver will change hands.

The entire job will be done in minutes. No one should be on the beach that night, and if there is, it is likely to be another small farmer. These people know how hard the last few years have been for Gerochus and won't run to the authorities with tales of illicit fig smuggling. No one wants the reputation of being an informer. Those that do are called 'sycophants' (literally 'fig-tellers'). They are not popular.

A city is privileged to have people prepared who prosecute law-breakers. I only wish the public were appropriately grateful. The reality is exactly opposite. Anyone who takes the personal risk of unpopularity for the public good is regarded as a sycophant rather than a patriot.

LYCURGUS *AGAINST LEOCRATES* 1.3

Business concluded for now, Gerochus is the first to leave. He finishes his wine and stands, casually looking around to see if anyone has been following the conversation. Pentarkes, the assistant tavernkeeper, is standing by the wine amphorae, a cloth in his hands and his face inscrutable in the lamplight. But that's no problem. Pentarkes and Phanagora know every second secret in the Piraeus. Gerochus smiles to himself as he walks down the darkened street for home. Maybe things will work out after all.

3RD HOUR OF THE NIGHT
(20.00–21.00)

THE SPARTAN SPY FINDS THE MOTHER LODE

Megistes makes no bones about being a Spartan. Since he can't go back to Sparta, however, he sees no point in enduring the privations of Spartiate life. Spartiates are Sparta's warrior class. They don't farm, trade or do anything but prepare for war. This involves regular physical exertion, icy-cold baths and food so unattractive that after trying it one visitor remarked thoughtfully, 'Now I understand why the Spartans do not fear death.'

Megistes was formerly a Spartiate. Then the outside world corrupted him. On a diplomatic mission to Thrace, Megistes realized that he liked wine that did not taste like vinegar, and blankets that did not feel like sheets of sandpaper. Albacore tuna cooked in cheese and honey was a world away from Sparta's notorious 'black broth', and Megistes liked that world. Accordingly, he started planning his retirement.

His diplomatic mission to Thrace involved taking a beautiful bowl of pure gold embossed with hunting scenes as a gift for a local king. Regrettably, the Athenians also had their plans for the kingdom, and had arranged for its pro-Spartan monarch to be assassinated.

The kingdom was under new management when Megistes arrived to a chilly reception. Under the circumstances the Spartan ambassador decided that there was no point in presenting the bowl to the new king. Instead he quietly sold the bowl to a local merchant for two little strongboxes packed with silver.

Then Megistes sent a slave with a message to Sparta saying that the Thracian king had actually received the bowl. Sadly, the king was assassinated a few days later. The bowl was gone, with nothing to show for Sparta's investment.

Then Megistes headed for Athens. Megistes intended to use his bounty to purchase a horse-breeding ranch in southern Italy, or a small villa adjacent to the fleshpots of Ephesus.

The Spartans made a bowl of bronze, with figures engraved around the outside rim. This had a capacity of 2,700 gallons. The intention was to make a gift of this in return for that present which Croesus had given them. But the bowl never got to Sardis [where Croesus had his palace].

...

The people of Samos [the island where the bowl ended up] say that the Spartans bringing the bowl arrived too late. When the ambassadors discovered that Sardis and Croesus had been taken [by the Persian army] they sold the bowl to private individuals in Samos, and these buyers dedicated it in the temple of Hera.

When the men who had sold the bowl returned to Sparta, they probably claimed that the Samians had stolen it.

HERODOTUS *HISTORIES* 1.70

Then, on the road to Athens, Megistes met a courier with a terse message from the Spartan authorities. He was to report back to Sparta immediately. Megistes quickly realized that the slave messenger he had sent ahead to Sparta must have betrayed him. All that awaited him in Sparta was trial, condemnation and quite possibly death. It had been a very valuable bowl.

Megistes became an exile. Since the Spartan authorities have a very long reach and a very short sense of humour, Megistes decided to stay in Athens, which is firmly anti-Spartan and with a few fleshpots of its own.

The tavern of Phanagora is hardly a sink of debauchery, but today Megistes has rented a room at the back for a private party. The advantage of this particular room is that it has a separate door opening into the alleyway through which, for example, young ladies can slip in discreetly without their fathers knowing.

Megistes is slightly late because he spent a few minutes observing the alleyway behind the tavern to make sure that no one had followed the person he is meeting. This person is no nubile wanton but a short, bald fellow with a perspiration problem.

'You're late,' he whines as Megistes pulls up a stool.

Megiste reaches into his tunic and drops a fist-sized leather bag on the table. It lands with a hefty thud, and the clink of coin settling. The bald man studies the bag with fearful, greedy attention until Megistes raises an impatient eyebrow.

The man carefully looks around the room, which contains nothing but a curtained-off cupboard, a table, a bench and an oil lamp. Satisfied, he unslings a satchel from his shoulder and pushes it across to Megistes.

'This has all got to be back in an hour.'

Megistes carefully opens the satchel while the bald man pulls back the cupboard curtain and removes a jar of wine and two clay cups. He pours the drinks, which Megistes ignores. This is it. The information that Sparta has spent so much time and gold to obtain.

The bald man is a senior clerk at the Arsenal. Within the Arsenal's cavernous halls Athenian warships are serviced. This is also where the records of the deployment of the Athenian triremes are kept, because it is convenient to keep the records with the ships.

Yet there's more, much more. Here is a list of accounts of military expenditures and budgets. And a list of allied forces,

SPARTAN WARRIORS EXERCISING AT THE RACECOURSE (*DROMOS*) AT SPARTA

and of the military reserves of Athenian subject states. Only years of Spartan discipline enables Megistes to keep his face impassive as he looks up from the treasure trove.

'Is this all?' he asks, as though this is not everything he was sent to find.

Megistes is a spy. Espionage in the Greek world is a hit-and-miss affair, but the Spartans are more professional than most. In fact, Megistes was trained for his role almost from boyhood. Over a century ago, Sparta took possession of the neighbouring state of Messenia, which it holds through fierce repression and terror.

Every year, the Spartans pick out those youths who most excel in the *agoge* – Sparta's brutal system of education for young warriors. The selected young men are enrolled into the *krypteia* – 'the secret ones'. The *krypteia*'s members are sent into the Messenian countryside as scouts and spies. They identify the Messenian leaders most respected in their villages and communities, and kill them. It does not really matter if their victims are pro- or anti-Spartan. The point is to keep the Messenians leaderless and terrified, and the *krypteia* does this job superbly.

The krypteia is wonderfully severe in toughening us up. Men go barefoot in winter and sleep without blankets. They have no attendants, but look after themselves as they roam the countryside, night and day.

THE SPARTAN MEGILLUS IN PLATO *LAWS* 633

Having shown their readiness to kill for Sparta, members of the *krypteia* are afterwards automatically appointed to the *hippeis*, the elite of the elite Spartiates. Every year five men retire from the *hippeis* and are dispatched on missions of reconnaissance and espionage. Megistes is one of those five.

Lichas was one of the Spartans called 'doers of good deeds'. These men are the five oldest of the hippeis, who retire each year. The year after they retire they are sent here and there by the Spartan state, unrelenting in their efforts.

HERODOTUS *HISTORIES* 1.67

The plan was always that Megistes should 'embezzle' the golden bowl and thus have a convincing reason for being in Athens. It was pure good fortune that the Thracian king had helped by getting himself assassinated. Megistes regards this as proof that Hermes, the god of con-men, merchants and spies, has personally blessed his operation.

This is a critical time for Sparta. The Spartans will never publicly admit it, but the Athenians convincingly won the recent war between the two states. Sparta intended the war to curb the growing Athenian empire, and Sparta failed. Today, Athens is more proud and powerful than ever.

Last year, rumours circulated that Athens was re-arming, and Sparta became very worried. Allegedly, the Athenians intend to invade Sicily. The Spartan authorities, however, are sceptical. What if the Athenian fleet suddenly swerves north as it reaches Cape Malea, and a huge, well-equipped army marches on unwalled Sparta? It is a chilling prospect.

On the other hand, perhaps the Athenians are daring and reckless enough to attack Sicily. In that case, with the Athenians hundreds of miles away, perhaps Sparta might launch a surprise attack of its own? It will only work if Athens is overstretched and vulnerable. Megistes has been placed in Athens to find out.

Other states frequently use merchants for espionage, but a trader from Sparta would be more suspicious than a declared spy. Sparta does not have a lot to trade. The state is agricultural and self-sufficient, its currency is unusable iron spits, and any Spartiate would rather disembowel himself than be involved in filthy commerce. Greed and corruption, however, are considered Sparta's secret vices, and Megistes carefully lived up to that stereotype while he infiltrated Athenian society.

Cyrus said, 'Now listen; there is a way that you do me a great kindness and your comrades a great service ... if you went to the enemy, pretending that you had fled from me, they would probably believe you ... Then you will come back to us, with complete information about the enemy's affairs. If I am right in my expectation, they will trust you and you can discover all their plans, so that you miss nothing of what we wish to know.'

XENOPHON *CYROPAEDIA* 6.38

Now he looks through the scrolls, secretly excited and appalled. So many men, a mighty fleet and so much gold!

He looks through the budget, noting the vast sums spent on bribing Sicilian politicians. Other spies have reported on the state of Syracuse's city walls and military preparedness. There are detailed descriptions of the main Sicilian harbours. The Athenians really mean their madcap plan.

Nicias and Lamarchus

Nicias was at this time in his mid-fifties. Born to an aristocratic family, he got along well with the like-minded Pericles who helped his rise to political prominence. The Athenian democracy was happy to vote aristocrats to high office provided they used their wealth and influence on behalf of the state. Nicias was a supporter of numerous public events, and sponsored at least one of the playwrights at the Great Dionysia.

Nicias was the type of general that the troops liked: cautious to a fault, and never risking lives in battle unless victory was almost certain. In this inter-war period of relative calm, Nicias is active in politics, trying to keep the peace he was largely responsible for brokering with the Spartans.

Nicias' main opponent was Alcibiades, who wanted a war to increase his personal reputation. Alcibiades was behind the bold plan to attack Sicily, a plan which Nicias opposed. As the incident just described illustrates, the Spartan 'peace' was packed with intrigue, both inter-city and domestic.

Lamarchus was an ally of Nicias. He was from a poor background, though this did not stop the Athenians from electing him as one of their generals.

That's the good news. Megistes flips through scroll after scroll, committing columns of figures to his trained memory. The bad news is that Athens has the men and resources to fight on two fronts, at least for a while. Megistes glances up from the scrolls at the bald clerk, who is already on to his third beaker of wine. 'These scrolls could be fake.'

'Check them for yourself,' says the clerk sullenly. 'I'm sure you have other sources.'

That is true, and actually Megistes is sure the scrolls are genuine. The entries are in different hands, and judging by the age of the ink and the papyrus, they go back years. Also, the most recent entry records the departure of a squadron of triremes for Thrace – a departure noted by Megistes' agents that very morning.

As he jots the most crucial details on a wax tablet, the spy comes to a decision. He will go to his rooms and spend the night writing what he has memorized. In the morning, he will visit his banker and retrieve for the Spartan state what silver coin he still has remaining. Then he will hurry to Sparta to present the information in person. The data he has obtained matter that much. In one swoop, Megistes has completed his mission.

He looks thoughtfully at the despicable little man who made all this possible. There is a curved dagger tucked behind the buckle of Megistes' belt, and he is a trained killer. But ... no. The clerk is needed to put the documents back exactly where they were taken from, or the Athenians will know their plans have been revealed. The clerk has been well paid and is not going to risk his life and his payment by talking. Let him live.

The clerk gathers the scrolls back into his satchel after Megistes has hurried from the room. The little man looks different now – deft and competent. 'You know,' he remarks to the empty air, 'for a moment, I thought he was going to try to silence me.'

There is a scraping noise as the wardrobe is moved aside, revealing a doorway into an adjoining room. Two men duck through and join the clerk. One of them, a fifty-ish bird-like fellow, says, 'And I hope you would have allowed him. We really need the Spartans to get that information.'

Pausanias

The scene of luring a spy into a room where he can be overheard by the authorities actually comes from a near-contemporary event in Sparta, recorded by Thucydides (*History of the Peloponnesian War* 1.133). The Spartan general Pausanias was colluding with the Persians. A go-between who carried messages to Persia invited the Spartan Euphors to listen from an adjoining chamber as he confronted Pausanias, and the authorities heard the man's guilt at first hand.

The second man, a veteran commander called Lamachus, looks unconvinced. Clearly, he feels that the whole performance is a roundabout way of doing things. If the Spartans wanted to know, and the Athenians want them to know, why not just tell them?

The reality is that it is not so simple. The Spartans are suspicious by nature, and Athens is trying hard to assuage those suspicions. Earlier in the afternoon the council sent a messenger telling the Spartans of Athenian intentions – but there's no certainty that the message will be believed. Anything the Athenians tell the Spartans about the size of their fleet, or the extent of their financial reserves will simply be dismissed as Athenian braggadocio. So the only way to be convincing is to let the Spartans find out for themselves.

It is Nicias' opinion that once the Spartans know that Athens is serious about invading Sicily, they'll stand back and hope that Athens and the Sicilians fight each other to a standstill. Then they'll aim to pounce on whatever is left. What worries him is that that's a viable strategy.

But he has done what he can. Hopefully, the Spartans are sufficiently convinced of Athenian strength to stay out of this round of warfare. As to Sicily – that's up to Alcibiades, and whatever fool they appoint to command with him. Nicias does not envy him, whoever he may be.

THE WEDDING GUEST EVICTS A TROUBLEMAKER

The hour is getting late, and Phormio wonders whether he should drop a hint to the bride's father that the wedding party should be moving on. Since the average Athenian wedding is a more than somewhat chaotic affair, it does not surprise the old soldier that the party is running late. Nevertheless, to some degree the lack of proper organization offends his tidy military mind.

In fact, reflects Phormio, the entire wedding is running late, as the occasion was originally scheduled for the month of Gamelion (late January/early February). Gamelion is an auspicious month to wed, because this is the month when Zeus, king of the gods, married his sister-wife Hera.

A marriage, however, is more than the union of a man and a woman. It is also the union of two families. The families in question are both reasonably wealthy landowners, and both fathers are friends of Phormio. Over the previous month Phormio has felt considerable sympathy for the frustration of the betrothed couple as he helped their fathers slowly navigate their way to an agreement on matters of tillage, inheritance, property and pasture rights. The actual betrothal was sorted out in an afternoon.

Eventually, the marriage was postponed to the end of the next month, Anthesterion. This is also a good month for weddings because it is the beginning of spring. More importantly from Phormio's personal perspective as a wedding guest, this is the month when the wine from the previous year's grape harvest has matured enough to be drinkable. The wine god Dionysus married an Anatolian queen in this month, so it too is auspicious from a religious viewpoint. Indeed, the city is in a party mood because of the three-day spring celebration, the Anthesteria, after which the month is named.

The wedding had been scheduled for the end of the month so as not to clash with that mid-month party. Then, deciding that they needed more time to prepare for the Dionysia, the city Archons had calmly clipped five days off Anthesterion and added them to Elaphebolion, the month in which the Dionysia takes place.

(The Archons could do this because the Athenian city calendar is a flexible affair to which days or even months can be added or deducted as the need arises. It's not unusual for the Archons to, for example, stretch out a month to give the army time to return to celebrate the harvest festivals. Spring came late this year, so Gamelion was extended to allow the Anthesteria celebrations to happen in the right climatic conditions. So even without the Dionysia, the month of Anthesterion needed trimming anyway if Elaphebolion was to start on time.)

As a result, it is now Elaphebolion, the month that honours Artemis, so the cakes at the wedding are stag-shaped. (The stag symbolizes Artemis, just as the owl symbolizes Athena, and the horse Poseidon.) The wine, however, is still young, plentiful and cheap. The abundance of drink has certainly added to the general air of festivity.

Sitting quietly in a corner that allows him to see the entire hall, Phormio notes young male guests have amused and irritated their elders with impromptu games, dances and wild, off-key singing. A youth called Hippoclides has imitated his namesake by dancing on the table in a handstand. This has generated a certain interest among the matrons present since, like all Athenian males, Hippoclides wears no underwear.

The Dance of Hippoclides

The dance of Hippoclides is related in Herodotus' *Histories* 6.129. The disapproving father-in-law was Psistratos, the ruler of Athens around 600 BC. When the original Hippoclides did a revealing tabletop dance, his father-in-law-to-be cancelled the planned wedding, saying, 'Hippoclides has danced away his bride.' To which the demoted bridegroom cheerfully replied, 'Hippoclides doesn't care.' There's now an Athenian catchphrase about whether a planned event goes forward or not – 'It's all the same to Hippoclides.'

Men and women are supposed to celebrate on different sides of the hall, but after the wedding meal (men eat first, then the women) a lot of informal mingling takes place. The men of marriageable age, however, have congregated around the wine krater. Phormio has a theory that this is for the same reason that cattle form a tight defensive cluster when hunted by wolves. The hunters in this case are the mothers of nubile daughters.

Phormio grins as he sees a young male stray too near the female side of the party. Within moments the youth will find himself pinned against a column, where hopeful mothers will politely but persistently grill him on his family connections, expectations and prospects. If deemed suitable, the man will then be treated to brief but heartfelt eulogies about the charms and domestic skills of the matrons' daughters.

The daughters themselves are considered too young to attend the festivities, the exception of course being the bride herself. She's the rosy-cheeked fifteen-year-old in a saffron dress sporting the short haircut that symbolizes her accession to married status. The bride's veil has already been ceremonially removed by the groom (the most significant part of the day's events as it demonstrates that the girl has been transferred to her new family), so there's nothing to shelter the over-lively young men at the wine krater from the bride's basilisk-like glare.

It is clear that someone has to intervene, so Phormio reluctantly volunteers himself for the task. On the pretext of refreshing his wine, he joins the group and says, 'A happy occasion this is, and by all means one we should celebrate. I commend your enthusiasm, but may I suggest you tone it down just a touch. The bride's family are getting a bit restless.'

He knows his advice will be taken. Athenian youngsters will respect any greybeard, and especially a veteran like himself with a scar across his face from a spear-thrust – a wound that also took away one eye. Also, he is Phormio, one of the better Athenian generals in the recent war. He is retired now, but his reputation as a warrior and sailor remains. (It is a point of quiet pride with him that when he was chosen for state office he was ineligible to take the position because he owed money.

The Assembly promptly gave him a minor task to perform, and then paid him exactly the sum of his debt – a mark of respect that he deeply values.)

Accordingly, when Phormio drops his hint, the young men disperse uncomplainingly. One man remains, somewhat truculently dipping his wine cup into the krater to refresh it and then making a sour grimace with his first swig.

Phormio

While a competent general and tactician, Phormio is best remembered today as a great Athenian admiral. Phormio won two naval battles against the Peloponnesians despite being outnumbered each time. His victories cemented Athenian naval supremacy on the Greek west coast. Nothing is heard of Phormio after 428 BC. It is thought that he died soon after fighting a land campaign in Acarnania, though, as suggested here, he may have been badly wounded and later retired.

Phormio guesses that the grimace is because the wine has been well diluted with water. As the saying goes, water the first krater for a formal gathering; half-mix the second, for a convivial affair; serve the third almost unwatered, for a proper party. By now the party should be getting on to the stronger wine. Instead the third krater has been well-watered, too – and the young man eyeing the huge urn disapprovingly is among the reasons why.

Over-indulgence is frowned upon at this stage, for this is still meant to be a formal gathering: the real party will kick off

BRIDESMAIDS PREPARE A BRIDE FOR HER BIG DAY

when the wedding procession arrives at the groom's house. Then the elderly guests will go off to bed and leave the night to the young men – not that they're having any trouble celebrating already.

It does occur to Phormio that by now they should have lit the torches and staggered into formation for the wedding procession. Still, the whole wedding has suffered continual delays since the engagement was first announced, so why should the final act be any different? Admittedly, the delay grates somewhat on his tidy military mind, but Phormio reminds himself that, firstly, he is not in charge and, secondly, wedding feasts are not military campaigns.

'You will remember this night fondly when you are camped outside the walls of Syracuse,' he informs the young man. The guest takes another swig of wine. 'Oh, yes. Alcibiades will show everyone how it's done.'

There's a feeling among the new crop of Athenian youths

that the generals of the last war had been pedestrian at best. Today, however, they claim Athens has a general with flair. Battle and diplomacy – Alcibiades can do both. The young men subscribe to the idea that the last war was only won because Demosthenes got lucky. But now, even if Athens has to fight the Spartans again, it will be an easy victory.

But Phormio disagrees. The Spartans are never easy. They weren't last time and they won't be next time. Yet Alcibiades has convinced the hotheads of Athens to follow him.

Last time, when the Spartans opened hostilities, no city anywhere was better prepared for war than Athens. The conflict was not an unexpected development and everything possible had been done to weather the storm. The trouble is that in military affairs no plan survives contact with reality unscathed.

Phormio remarks as much to the young man, who hoots derisively. 'Yes, Pericles. What a plan!' He says the name 'Pericles' as though it leaves a bad taste in his mouth.

Pericles' plan was that Athens should not fight the Spartans in Attica. Instead he persuaded the rural population to retreat into Athens and wait behind the safety of the city walls while the Spartans prowled the fields outside. They might devastate the crops, but Athens could easily survive on grain imported from the Euxine.

The young man slams his wine cup down on the table so hard that a fountain splashes up from its centre. 'Pericles got it wrong!'

It is true that Pericles might have foreseen the plague. After all, when you pack tens of thousands of extra people into a city, into every courtyard and gutter, as Pericles did with refugees from the countryside, disease is a likely consequence.

And when Athenian strategy is based on inviting ships from all over the world to import foods and, with that food, whatever diseases they're carrying, then illness becomes almost certain. As masterplans go, the one dreamed up by Pericles certainly had some major flaws.

The young man leans forward suddenly, causing Phormio to flinch from his wine-laden breath.

'Pericles is the father of Athens' misfortune!'

'Please keep your voice down,' says Phormio sharply, 'or we might need to step out for a bit of fresh air. The wine seems to be getting to you.'

This is a wedding feast, he thinks, and a joyous occasion is hardly time to discuss topics like plague – especially *that* plague. Pericles didn't see it coming, and the plague killed him, along with thousands of Athenians. The planned attack on Thrace was cancelled because afterwards Athens hardly had an army left. It was all they could do to keep the navy going, and they needed that navy to survive.

Until the plague, it was one of the healthiest of years for Athens. Then the disease hit the Piraeus. Brought from Egypt, it took the strong and the weak alike, young and old. It didn't matter whether you went to a doctor, or prayed at a temple, or did nothing. You died, or you survived – and survivors believed that no disease could kill them after that.

Aside from the threat to life, the plague threw the city into total anarchy. Athenians committed crimes – robberies, rape and murder – believing they wouldn't live long enough to be punished for them. And nobody bothered to maintain order, as there seemed little point. There was a greater judgement on the way; they might as well enjoy what time they had left.

Phormio estimates the youth would have been about fourteen then. A pretty boy, making him a likely victim for any sexual predators he met on the street. Although he wouldn't have wanted to leave the house anyway – there would have been corpses lying unburied in the gutters, and dogs tearing at them until the plague killed the dogs as well. Funeral pyres were started right there in the street using smashed-up furniture and household timber. And while funeral rites were going on, others would add more bodies to the fire.

Phormio was not alone in noting that the plague never hurt Sparta. The Spartans live spread out in villages and that warlike nation never had the need to pack everyone from all those villages into one city in the middle of summer. Perhaps it would have been better to do with the villagers as the Athenians had done with their livestock and evacuate everyone to the nearby island of Euboea.

Phormio turns his thoughts from past troubles to the present problem. 'Pericles …' he starts to say, but the youth shouts him down.

'Pericles! He was an awful strategist, an awful general, and a rotten person! He … Let go of me!'

The Plague

The plague that hit Athens in the summer of 430 BC was a terrible event which killed an estimated third of the population sheltering behind the city walls. A mass grave from the period suggests that the plague was two concurrent epidemics, one of which was a mutant form of typhoid fever. We have an eyewitness account of the plague in Athens, for Thucydides was there, became ill, but recovered. The description of the plague here is lifted mostly verbatim from Thucydides' *History of the Peloponnesian War* 2.47.1

Phormio has taken the young man by one arm. He exchanges looks with another burly guest who has taken the other arm. The man was shouting, and they had made an earlier agreement that if he upset the other guests, it would be time to pitch him on to the cobblestones outside.

The young man struggles violently as he is lifted, and kicks at Phormio's shins. Since he is barefoot, this achieves nothing apart from hurting his toes. The other party-goers carefully pay no attention as the writhing body makes its way to the entrance. The disturbance has achieved one thing, though. Everyone has been sufficiently distracted from socializing, drinking or enjoying the banqueting dishes for a rough consensus to form that it's time to get the wedding procession started. A laughing, jostling throng starts flowing out of the hall into the courtyard.

Leaving the drunken young man to pull himself together, Phormio joins the group around the bride – who, he notes, seems more than a bit apprehensive about the rest of her wedding night. Nevertheless, she must be relieved that it's finally going to happen. Seeing Phormio return, the bride asks, 'Was the plague as bad as that man was saying? He seemed really upset.'

'We shouldn't discuss such things at your wedding. But, yes, I understand it was horrible. Pericles' son feels somehow responsible. That's why he acts the way he does. No one else blames him, but for some reason he blames himself. This isn't the first social event where he's drunk too much and been thrown out.'

Pericles the Younger

The illegitimate son of Pericles and Aspasia was originally banned from Athenian citizenship as a result of a law his own father had carried. In an ambiguous sentence, Plutarch also suggests that the elder Pericles might have molested his son's wife. In any case, his 'harlot-birth' (as Eupolis the poet put it, according to Plutarch's *Life of Pericles* 24) seems to have embittered the son. He was later legitimized by the Athenian Assembly. When war with Sparta resumed, he was among the commanders who won an epic naval victory against the Peloponnesians. The Athenians executed him anyway, because after the battle a storm was brewing and Pericles the younger ordered the triremes to safety without stopping to pick up survivors in the water.

THE BRIDE TRAVELS TO HER NEW HOME

The procession is outside. Torches flare and shouted jokes split the night, answered by yells from nearby houses as the sleepy occupants protest the noise. No one is seriously annoyed, though. Raucous wedding processions are a fact of Athenian life, and generally welcomed by the community as a whole.

Phaedra and her parents leave the hall. At the door her husband is waiting to complete another of the steps that will seal their marriage. There is no 'I do' moment in an Athenian wedding. Rather, the process started with the engagement and continued when the couple took a ritual bath of purification that morning. They became more married as the day went on, the most important moment being the ceremonial lifting of Phaedra's veil.

Now, the groom seizes Phaedra's forearm, wrenching her from her mother, who steps aside. This 'capture' of the bride comes from a prehistoric time when brides were literally taken in raids or as prisoners of war. Phaedra's father formally recognizes the change of guardianship: 'With those here as witness, I now give you this maiden in marriage that you may have children together.'

That's it. This is no longer Phaedra's home. Her childhood toys are gone, given away or sacrificed to the goddess. She is now the mistress of her own home, where her mother-in-law is waiting to welcome her. Phaedra is pleased that this house is close to her own – close to the house that was once hers, she firmly reminds herself.

Phaedra has been impatient to marry for years now – she will be sixteen soon. Most of her childhood friends have long been married, and on their visits her mother treated them as near-equals, while she remained a child.

Phaedra will boss her own household (she has been taking lessons from her mother) and in a few years she will have her own brood of children.

All she knows of those children's father is that he is Caendies, son of Agoron. He has no physical defects and is the only remaining child in his family, having lost a brother in the disastrous battle at Mantinea last year. That loss helped to get Phaedra married at last. The parents of Caendies had just one son remaining in an uncertain world. Therefore it was time to get started on grandchildren, lest their family perish altogether.

The other thing Phaedra knows is that with this marriage Caendies has gained his family two acres of prime farmland in the *deme* of Kephisia, close to his family's other land holdings. It was the proximity of the family lands, above all else, that led to today's marriage.

Phaedra hopes that her new husband will spend maximum time out in the fields and minimal time interfering with her household. Apart from the sex, of course. He has to be home for that. Phaedra wants to know lots more about the sex. She gives a shy, yet thoughtful look at the man who still holds her tentatively by the arm as he guides her into the courtyard and into a noisy shower of the traditional fruit and nuts.

Before them stands the mule-cart that will carry Phaedra to her new home. She knows that the axle is a bit suspect because she heard her father worrying about it before the ceremony. Made from an applewood off-cut, it is intended for just the one trip. When she reaches her new home Phaedra will burn that axle as a sign that there is no going back.

Thereafter, her next public appearance will probably be her husband's funeral. Since Caendies is almost twice Phaedra's age she feels certain to outlive him, even if an enemy spear doesn't get him before old age does. As to her own mortality, Phaedra has heard dark whispers from friends about the dangers of childbirth. But given that she has hips wide as a barn door, she feels no worry about predeceasing her husband on that account.

The procession swings on to the street, with Phaedra's mother alongside the cart holding high two torches, as is traditional. Beside her sits her new husband, who says nothing. Phaedra will later discover that this is because he is almost paralysed with terror. A new home, wife and household is a big step for him, too. The silence of the spouse allows the bride to eavesdrop on a shouted conversation between her mother and an aristocratic friend called Xanthippe. ('What kind of parents name their daughter Yellow Horse?' she wonders.)

'No, he isn't here. Obviously, because I am.' The cart lurches, throwing Phaedra against her husband. She is so preoccupied with his close proximity that she misses her mother's reply. Xanthippe speaks again.

'A symposium spouting quips which sound wise to the drunken, and drunken to the wise. I promised your husband he would be here. But if I tell Socrates to do something, he does the opposite. Curse him!'

Again Phaedra misses the next bit of the conversation

because a friend of the groom comes alongside and shouts some innuendo that Phaedra does not understand. It is evidently obscene, because there is a degree of violence in the 'friendly' cuff her husband gives in reply.

Xanthippe is recalling her recent dinner – a meal that became the talk of Athens. Socrates had spontaneously invited a group of friends to his home, confidently assuming that Xanthippe could put together a dinner for six at a moment's notice. Regrettably, the household larder contained nothing but a few vegetables and a rack of lamb.

Xanthippe had complained bitterly that even if she went hungry, this wasn't enough for a decent meal for the guests. 'If they're good friends, they won't care,' said Socrates. 'If they are not good friends, then I don't care.'

Socrates didn't think to ask if Xanthippe cared, even if it was her reputation as a housekeeper at stake. Phaedra reflects that, while exceptional in many ways, Socrates is still an Athenian male.

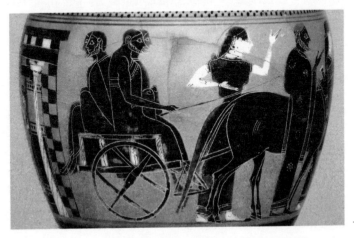

WEDDING REVELLERS HITCH A RIDE ON THE BRIDAL CART

Xanthippe explains to Phaedra's mother that, contrary to rumour, the pair didn't fight about it. As Socrates often says, it takes two people for a fight, and he doesn't fight with his wife. On this occasion, the more Xanthippe had screamed at Socrates the more reasonable Socrates became. Finally, Xanthippe had thrown him out of the house before she brained him with an urn.

Phaedra looks to see how her mother reacts to the astounding (but wonderful) idea of a wife throwing her husband out of the house. Sadly, her mother is turned away and she can only see the vine-wreathed bun at the back of her head. Xanthippe's face is earnest in the torchlight as she continues to try to explain the exasperations of life with the man they call the 'gadfly of Athens'.

So, Socrates was on a bench in the courtyard. From upstairs Xanthippe could see that he had started up a conversation with some admirers who just wandered in off the street. He was about to invite them to dinner as well, so what could Xanthippe do? She was carrying a bucket of water, so she just tipped it. Over his head.

Phaedra's mother looks at Xanthippe in amazement. 'How did Socrates take it?'

'You haven't heard?' asks Xanthippe sourly. 'He just looked up, and remarked, "Well, after the thunder, you can expect rain." Since then everyone repeats that back at me – which hurts more than if he had taken a stick to my buttocks. But Socrates would not hit me. He's too *gentle*.' That last word is uttered with venom.

The conversation continues, but high on her mule-cart, Phaedra sees something else. They are on a narrow street alongside the Eridanus, and there are some twenty torches winding towards them. The two advancing groups exchange shouts and mock-threats. The wedding party has run into a *komos*, a common danger when you leave the wedding procession until late.

A *komos* is a street party on the move. Usually the group is made up of young aristocrats and their retainers. Sometimes it is because they have become drunk enough for one household to evict them and they have staggered off to inflict themselves on some unsuspecting friend. Or perhaps the entire party has decamped to merge with another party across town. Either way, everyone gives precedence to a wedding procession. The *komos* should now step aside.

Instead, Phaedra's husband groans with a mixture of resignation and dread. 'Oh, by Athena's grace! Please, no. Not Alcibiades.'

A young man shoulders through the crowd, a garland of ivy and violets askew on his beribboned head, copper curls of hair shining in the torchlight. He looks at Phaedra with a wide, happy smile and gives her an elegantly over-exaggerated salutation. Phaedra giggles and hides her face. So, this is the notorious Alcibiades. He looks much younger than she would have imagined. Her parents are stony-faced, while Xanthippe gives Alcibiades an outright glare. Alcibiades now ignores the blushing bride and turns his attention to Xanthippe, asking her solicitously, 'I trust you have recovered from your recent disastrous dinner party. Did Socrates get the cake I sent so that he wouldn't starve?'

Phaedra knows what happened to that cake. Almost certainly Alcibiades does, too. When it comes to Socrates, the Athenian rumour mill is very efficient. Xanthippe had taken the cake and trampled it into the street. Afterwards the dogs ate what was left.

Socrates was philosophical about the entire incident. He

had just shrugged and asked if Xanthippe realized that she had trampled her share of the cake as well. Now the fuming Xanthippe takes a half-step towards Alcibiades. Phaedra is somewhat relieved that Xanthippe has no weapons near to hand. In her current mood, she would probably use them.

Xanthippe

Most of the interactions between Xanthippe and Socrates come verbatim from Diogenes Laërtius' *Lives and Opinions of the Eminent Philosophers*, Book 5 passim, though the trampling of Alcibiades' cake comes from Aelian's *Assorted Histories* 12.12. The feuding couple never divorced because they seemed, despite everything, to actually love each other. Socrates frequently defended Xanthippe, and she was completely distraught at his execution, as seen in Plato's *Phaedo* 60.

'This is not well,' says one of the older men angrily. 'Alcibiades, tell your party to stand aside.' The speaker is Hipponicus, a man of great reputation and wealth. Phaedra's mother had been in ecstasies when he accepted the wedding invitation. Even Alcibiades seems impressed. Giving Phaedra a wave, he returns to his group who greet him with laughter.

'What does he want now?' asks Caendies suddenly. Alcibiades has turned around, and is walking back to Hipponicus with a strange smile on his face. Swiftly and unexpectedly, Alcibiades hits Hipponicus hard, sending the man crumpling to the ground. A whoop goes up from Alcibiades' retinue, while the wedding party watch, appalled.

'Why did you do that?' demands Phaedra's father. Even Alcibiades seems surprised by his action. He rubs his fist.

'I didn't have any quarrel with him,' he explains. 'I wasn't angry. It was just for the joke of the thing.' Alcibiades gestures at his friends, who are doubled up with laughter. 'They dared me.'

A nephew of Hipponicus lunges forward and the companions of Alcibiades rush to their leader's defence. The young men of the wedding party cast aside their torches and spring into battle. Within moments, the shadowy street is filled with brawling, cursing men and screaming women. Phaedra sits above the fray and watches it all with open-mouthed fascination. Who could have imagined that married life was so exciting?

The street battle lasts less than a minute before a new force joins the fight. These are lean, tattooed men wielding short whips with ruthless efficiency. Though fewer than a dozen, these are sober and experienced practitioners of violence, which they use unhesitatingly on anyone who shows the slightest bellicosity. Soon half of the banqueters are hog-tied in the street alongside bruised and complaining young men from the wedding party. Discarded torches splutter in the mud beside trampled garlands.

The Scythian archers who have so brutally restored order are the Athenian equivalent of a police force. Their commander is a stocky official from the Athenian Assembly. He comes over to give a report to Phormio, and the old general listens innocently, his left hand discreetly covering the bleeding knuckles on his right. The official nods at the remnants of the *komos* procession.

'Been expecting trouble from this lot, sir. So we were following at a discreet distance. Sorry about your group's

> *He once struck Hipponicus a blow with his fist – Hipponicus,*
> *the father of Callias, a man of great reputation through his*
> *family and influence owing to his wealth. He had no quarrel*
> *with him, nor was he afflicted with anger, but simply as a*
> *joke, on a bet with his friends.*
>
> PLUTARCH *LIFE OF ALCIBIADES* 8

young men. We'll give it a half-hour and cut everyone loose. They can rejoin your party later. Just keep it indoors, please.'

Xanthippe has been examining the prisoners (and Phaedra notes that she gave one of them a hearty kick when she thought no one was looking). She asks, 'Where's Alcibiades?'

'That's one thing about that young man,' says Phormio dryly. 'When all the trouble he's caused is over, when the dust has settled and it's time to face the consequences, then Alcibiades is never there.'

Scythian Archers

It is believed that these were introduced by Pericles. Their job was to maintain order in the streets and to act as enforcers for Athenian officials. In Aristophanes (*Assemblywomen* 143), we see them trying (and failing) to subdue an unruly crowd. 'My archer force came off badly,' admits the magistrate. They are more successful later, when a spectator comments, 'You can see the archers dragging more than one unruly drunk out of the marketplace.'

THE SWORD-DANCER
GROWS AMOROUS

A riadne is in the garden doing stretching drills while her boyfriend Demetrios moves his supple body through a series of complex dance moves, eyes closed as he dances to a rhythm that only he can hear. Tyche, the flute player, is silently fingering the notes – she will play later, but for now the troupe do not want to disturb the diners at their meal.

Their manager, known to everyone – and by now probably also to himself – as 'the Syracusan', sticks his head out of the door. 'They're taking away the tables. Get ready.'

Ariadne and her companions are the entertainment at tonight's symposium. It's a high-class affair and correspondingly well-paid. The Syracusan has given them a brief run-down on those present. Their host is Callias, one of the most powerful politicians in Athens. There's a trophy-winning athlete called Autolycus, a philosopher called Socrates, Nicoratus, son of Nicias the politician, and a minor aristocrat called Agathon who is accompanied by two friends. There are also three *hetarias*, one of whom has already called for stronger wine.

The flute girl makes a face when she hears the number of *hetarias* present. Unless two men pair up they'll be a girl short if – as very often happens – the proceedings degenerate into a full-scale orgy. The flute girl will be expected to make up the numbers, and even with a generous gratuity afterwards, it's not her ideal end to the evening. She considers herself a musician (a very good one), not a courtesan.

'Don't worry,' the Syracusan assures her. 'The *hetarias* generally know to stay reasonably sober and at least one of the men will pass out, so that will shorten the odds. Now get ready – they've started the hymn.' (Symposium diners customarily start the second part of their evening with a libation and a hymn to the gods. Then the serious drinking begins. 'Symposium', after all, literally translates as 'drinking together'.)

As the hymn ends, the three troop into the *andron*, the men's room of the house, where the manager introduces them. 'First, our flute girl, perfect in her playing. Next, a skilled dancing girl, wonderfully excellent in her art. And here in the bloom of his youthful beauty, a boy who dances with matchless grace.'

Tyche is passing Ariadne the hoops which she will be juggling, when there is a thunderous knocking on the street door. Frowning, Callias sends servants to investigate. 'If they are friends, invite them in; otherwise, say that the symposium has finished.'

Moments later a drunken voice bellows from the courtyard, 'Where is Agathon? Take me to Agathon!' and at length Alcibiades staggers in, supported between two servants.

'Greetings, friends,' he says from the doorway. 'Will you have a very drunken man join you at the party? Or shall I give this garland to Agathon, which was why I came here, and be on my way? Let me take this garland from my own head and crown this fairest and wisest of men.

'Are you laughing at me because I am drunk? Yes, laugh, but I know that I am speaking the truth. But first tell me; do we have an understanding? Will you drink with me or not?'

With everyone urging him in, Alcibiades effortlessly takes over the proceedings. 'You are far too sober, my friends. Completely unacceptable. The agreement under which I was allowed in was that we get drinking together. I elect myself master of the feast until you are all well drunk.

'Give me a large wine cup. No, you servant, bring me that wine cooler.' The wine cooler is a vase usually holding chilled water to cool and dilute the wine of the guests. Filled with wine, it makes a substantial drink. Alcibiades drains it without pausing.

Swaying markedly, he orders the servant, 'Fill it again for Socrates. Though you will observe, my friends, that this clever trick is wasted on him. He will soak up the lot and get no nearer to being drunk.'

Without comment, Socrates also drains the vase.

Finally, Ariadne can begin her act. Tyche plays with an exaggerated rhythm to help Ariadne keep time. The men – veteran soldiers all – recognize it as a well-known marching song and lustily supply the words. Demetrios passes three more hoops to join the six that Ariadne is juggling, casting them almost as high as the rafters. For that extra bit of showmanship, she dances below the hoops as she catches and casts, keeping perfect time.

The delighted spectators roar their approval, but Ariadne is so absorbed in concentration she hardly notices. She throws one hoop that little bit higher and without looking catches the extra hoop that Demetrios throws to her. Ten hoops, and the applause picks up. Higher … higher … till the hoops graze the ceiling. Still dancing, Ariadne nods twice – signalling Demetrios that she can do two more.

THE MUSICIAN'S ELEGANT DRESS AND HARP SUGGEST
SHE HAS LANDED A HIGH-PAYING GIG

Beat, catch, throw. Catch the final hoop, throw, step, throw – there's twelve hoops on the go now, and Ariadne's timing is getting ragged. So as the hoops come down she flicks them aside to Demetrios who stacks each arrival on the table beside him. Now Tyche takes her timing from Ariadne and wraps up her tune just as the last hoop is placed on the table. Panting slightly, Ariadne takes a bow.

Socrates leads the applause, gently moving the head of a slumbering Alcibiades from the crook of his arm in order to do so. He remarks, 'Gentlemen, this girl shows by her performance that a woman's nature is every bit equal to a man's. And this is but one further proof among many. All a girl lacks is strength and (being younger) judgement. Those of you who have wives should be encouraged to teach them what you can, so they may be true partners.'

One of the drinkers makes the obvious rejoinder. 'If that's your opinion, Socrates, why not tutor your own wife? It seems you let your Yellow Horse remain as wild and savage as any wife and, indeed I imagine, as any wife that will ever be.'

'Well,' replies Socrates, 'I shall follow your metaphor. The rider who wishes to become an expert horseman says, "I want no docile animal, broken to the bridle. My horse needs to be a creature with spirit." He feels that if he can manage such an animal then every other horse will be child's play.

'In my case, I wish to be among people, and I teach human beings. And so I choose to live with a high-spirited wife, since if I can get along with her I can certainly get along with the rest of humanity.'

While this exchange is going on, a large hoop is brought out and presented with a flourish. The hoop is almost the height of Ariadne, lined with sword blades that point inwards, leaving a small gap in the middle. Demetrios holds one side of the hoop, the Syracusan another, and Tyche picks up the pace on her flute.

Before the audience can fully grasp the point of all this, Ariadne launches herself through the ring of swords, landing in a forward roll. She pulls off her tunic, revealing a very short skirt and tightly bound breasts. Then she somersaults through the ring, feeling one of the sword points lightly graze her ankle. On landing she glances down and checks her feet are set *exactly* right, then does a backflip, bringing up her feet as soon as she is through the hoop, so that she lands on her hands. After a tense moment, she pushes down, and flips herself to her feet through the hoop.

Ariadne quickly repeats this thrice, until the fearful spectators beg her to stop. Then, coolly and without mishap, she performs a series of forward and backward somersaults through the ring, completing her performance to an awed silence that is even better than applause.

'Okay,' says Socrates eventually, 'now that you have seen a girl – hardly yet a woman – launch herself so boldly among those swords, can you ever again deny that courage comes from training; that it can be taught?'

'Indeed not,' someone replies feelingly. 'No, our friend the Syracusan should tell the Athenian authorities that – for a substantial price – he is prepared to give the whole Athenian people courage to face enemy spears at close range. That dancing girl is proof he can do it.'

It's time for Ariadne to take a break, so she retires to wash while Demetrios entertains with his sinuous dances, weaving bonelessly as a snake while Tyche plays a haunting tune on her flute. Bathed and re-dressed, Ariadne relaxes to the music.

She is roused by the sound of laughter. Pleasure, surprise and even lust – she is used to such feelings being expressed when Demetrios dances. But mirth? She peeks out and discovers that Demetrios is taking a break. Instead, Socrates is twisting erotically on the floor, beard waggling in counter-time to his wobbling paunch. Tyche is trying to keep a tune, but keeps breaking into unprofessional fits of giggles.

'What?' Socrates reproves the room, his expression serious. 'It pleases you all to laugh. Is it funny that I want to improve my health by exercise, and so eat and sleep better? I don't want to be a runner, with bulging legs and skinny shoulders, nor a boxer who builds his shoulders at the expense of his legs. Dancing distributes the exercise across the body, allowing for even development.'

He gives a twirl.

'Or is it funny that in future I shall need no wrestling

partner at the gymnasium? Indeed, I'll no longer have to strip my old body in public. I shall exercise indoors in winter, and in the shade during the summer heat. And yet you laugh. Is it at my desire to slim down this somewhat over-developed belly? Is that the reason?'

He turns to the Syracusan. 'Breathtaking as it is, throwing somersaults around sword points is a display of danger not entirely suited to the present mood of the party. Can you persuade your young people to perhaps assay some pantomime in dance? I think they themselves might enjoy that, and in the process lend our festivity the grace and charm I have apparently failed to supply.'

'Excellent idea!' exclaims the Syracusan. 'Just give me a moment.' He rushes to the back room where Tyche, Demetrios and Ariadne are already in an excited huddle. It takes only a few moments to come up with a theme inspired by Ariadne's namesake, Ariadne of Crete, the daughter of King Minos.

As everyone in the audience knows, this Ariadne was instrumental in helping Theseus slay the Minotaur by giving him the golden thread that guided him through the labyrinth. Thereafter, Theseus and Ariadne eloped from Crete, only for the faithless Theseus to abandon his lover on the island of Naxos. Yet Ariadne had the last laugh, for the desolate maiden was seen by the god Dionysus, who took her for his bride.

The dance will enact the moment after the wedding when Dionysus, having ushered out the last guests, comes to claim his bride.

The audience watches intently as Ariadne seats herself on a makeshift throne while Tyche strikes up a Bacchic revel. Ariadne remains seated, but her anticipation is clear.

Demetrios dances lightly to her, tenderly embracing, and with feigned bashfulness Ariadne wraps her arms around him, both swaying to the time of the music. Demetrios lifts her to her feet and the pair dance, sometimes in a close embrace, sometimes springing balletically free.

Demetrios and Ariadne are perfectly paired: young, athletic and beautiful. As the dance goes on, it slowly dawns on the audience that the passion is not faked – actually the two have forgotten the spectators and are dancing for themselves alone. This is no pantomime but two young people doing what they have long set their hearts upon.

'Do you love me?' whispers Demetrios as he bends Ariadne back in an embrace.

'I do,' she assures him earnestly.

The Symposium

This final hour of the symposium is a collaborative effort by Plato, Xenophon and myself. The major contributor is Xenophon, and the classicist will recognize most of his *Symposium* Book IX with the philosophical badinage removed. Ariadne's sword dancing, the less elegant endeavours of Socrates and the final dance of Ariadne and Demetrios are as described by Xenophon.

Plato's contribution is the arrival of Alcibiades, fresh, as I imagine, from his escapade in the alleyway. Alcibiades spends the rest of Plato's symposium being his usual obnoxious self, so I have quietly stunned him and given the floor to Socrates and Ariadne. My own contribution has been to add continuity, edit and translate. After all, when you have actual eyewitness reports there is little else to add.

Catching her in his arms, Demetrios expertly whirls her to the back room where a friendly chair awaits. They are unaware that the midnight hour has just passed, just as they are unheeding of the guests at the dinner party, whom they leave to start the coming day in whatever manner they please.

EPILOGUE

Alcibiades got his Sicilian expedition and led a massive fleet and army against the city of Syracuse. Soon afterwards he was relieved of command and recalled to Athens where his enemies had accused him of blasphemy. Command fell to Nicias who had been unenthusiastic about the project from the start.

After a number of severe setbacks, the Athenians – typically – doubled down on their effort and sent to Sicily an even larger fleet and army. The entire force was totally destroyed in one of the greatest of Greek military debacles.

The Spartans took advantage of Athenian weakness and declared war. They were flush with money supplied by the Persians, and primed on the strategic weaknesses of Athens by the vindictive Alcibiades, who chose not to return to Athens.

Athens fought hard and to the end, but after almost a decade of bitter fighting the city lost its last fleet and army. Besieged and helpless, Athens was forced to surrender to the Spartans. The city walls were thrown down yet again, and the abominable Critias was put in charge as a Spartan puppet.

Athens being Athens, the city bounced back again. After a brisk revolution, the democracy was restored and the city walls rebuilt once more. Athens resumed thumbing its nose at Sparta and supplying the world with orators and philosophers.

But it was never quite the same.

ENDNOTES

1. Homer, *Iliad* 1.528

2. Aristophanes, *Knights* passim

3. Thucydides, *History of the Peloponnesian War* 6.31

4. This is why there will be no trireme shipwrecks for future archaeologists to study.

5. Thucydides, *History of the Peloponnesian War* 5.89, following Dutton trans. 1910

6. The shape of the latter will give later eras the word 'crater'.

7. Philosophumena of Hippolytus 4.35

8. 'Dismissal of Spirits', *Papyri Graecae Magicae* 4.915

9. Xenophon, *Memorabilia* 3.12

10. Diogenes Laërtius, *Plato* 3.7

11. Even today, this is called a 'Hippocrates bandage'.

12. Homer, *Odyssey* 19, 138

13. This isn't in fact a quote, but a five-word summary of a notably longer piece of text. Euphiletos, who has murdered Eratosthenes, is trying to justify his actions to the jury. Euphiletos claims that Eratosthenes was having an affair with his wife, that he caught them in the act, before killing Eratosthenes as the law permits. Eratosthenes' family claim that this is a lie to cover up a premeditated murder. Euphiletos has a vested interest in attempting to portray adultery as

worse than rape because 'I was punishing an adulterer' is his defence.

14. The oldest source for this variant is Euripides' *Iphigenia at Aulis*, written 408-6 BC. The addition of this element would not be out of place for Euripides, who we know made other significant contributions to myth.

15. The incident with the cloak is from a lost text called the *Historical Commentaries* of Hieronymus of Rhodes, quoted in Athenaeus, complete with Sophocles' indignant little poem in *Deipnosophists* 13.82.

16. Thrasyllos, the mad boat-spotter, was a real character. His condition was related by the writer Heraclides in a text called *On Pleasure* and quoted in Athenaeus, *Deipnosophists* 12.81.

17. What we would call a dark red wine, the Greeks called 'black' because that's how it looks in a clay mug by lamplight. This is why Homer can refer to the 'wine-dark sea' in his poetry.

18. Here, I have put Aristotle's arguments against Hippodamus into the mouth of Socrates, as that's probably whence they originally came.

19. Xenophon, *Hellenica* 2.4.11

20. In fact, this crack was made by the courtesan Gnathaena to the playwright Diphilius, quoted in Athenaeus *Deipnosophists* 13.43.

21. All this advice is extracted from Lucian's *Dialogues of the Courtesans*.

22. Alciphron, *Letters* 34

23. Quoted mainly from 'Petale to Simaleon', Alciphron, *Letters* 57.

24. This idea of the origin of the Venus symbol is from the nineteenth century. The folk idea behind the Mars symbol is

much older, but equally dubious. The more commonly accepted idea is that the symbols developed from the letters phi (for female) and theta (for male) based on the fact that theta is the first letter of the Greek name for the planet Mars, and phi the first letter of the Greek name for the planet Venus.

25. Aristophanes, *Archanians* 1530

Picture Credits

Page 17: Lorado Taft's miniature set of the workshop of sculptor Phidias. Photograph courtesy of the University of Illinois Archives.

Page 27: Thalia, Muse of Comedy, from the Sarcophagus of the Muses, Louvre Museum, Paris / Marie-Lan Nguyen, Wikimedia Commons, Public Domain.

Page 39: © The Trustees of the British Museum.

Page 47: Lenormant Trireme Relief, Acropolis Museum, Athens / Marsyas, Wikimedia Commons, CC BY-SA 2.5.

Page 62: Athenian silver tetradrachm, Cabinet des Médailles, Bibliothèque Nationale, Paris / Marie-Lan Nguyen, Wikimedia Commons, CC BY-SA 2.5.

Page 69: DeAgostini / Getty Images.

Page 78: The LIFE Picture Collection / Getty Images.

Page 88: Mosaic from Pompeii, Museo Archeologico Nazionale, Naples / Marie-Lan Nguyen, Wikimedia Commons, Public Domain.

Page 99: Red-figure krater (ceramic), Greek, (fourth century BC) / Museo Archeologico, Cefalu, Sicily, Italy / Bridgeman Images.

Page 108: Achilles bandaging the arm of the wounded Patroclus. Ink drawing after an Attic cup by the potter Sosias, *ca.* 500 BC, Altes Museum, Berlin / Wellcome Foundation CC BY 4.0.

Page 119: Terracotta statuette of a woman, first half of fifth century BC / Bequest of Walter C. Baker, 1971, Metropolitan Museum of Art, New York.

Page 133: Horsemen from the west frieze of the Parthenon, *ca.* 477–433 BC, British Museum / Marie-Lan Nguyen, Wikimedia Commons, Public Domain.

Page 142: Details of hoplites on the Chigi vase (reconstruction) / Phokion, Wikimedia Commons, CC BY-SA 4.0.

Page 152: *Phryne Before the Areopagus*, Jean-Baptiste Dehays (French, Colleville 1729–65 Paris / Rogers Fund, 1961, Metropolitan Museum of Art, New York

Page 158: *Der Siegesbote von Marathon*, bronze, Max Kruse, 1884, Nationalgalerie, Berlin / akg-images.

Page 170: Map of the Long Walls from *Athens and its Monuments* by Charles Head Weller, Macmillan, New York 1913.

Page 183: Falkensteinfoto / Alamy.

Page 186: Terracotta lamp, fifth-fourth century BC / J. Paul Getty Museum.

Page 199: Interior of Attic red-figured kylix, *ca.* 490 BC, British Museum, London / Marie-Lan Nguyen, Wikimedia Commons / Public Domain.

Page 209: Woodcut from *Hellas und Rom* by Jakob von Falke, W. Spemann, Stuttgart 1879 / akg-images.

Page 217: Granger / REX / Shutterstock.

Page 230: Terracotta nuptial lebes attributed to the Naples Painter / Rogers Fund, 1906, Metrapolitan Museum of Art, New York.

Page 239: Terracotta lekythos attributed to the Amasis Painter, *ca.* 550–530 BC / Purchase, Walter C. Baker Gift, 1956, Metropolitan Museum of Art, New York.

Page 248: Photograph © Philip Matyszak.

Bibliography

Modern texts used in preparation of this manuscript

Camp, J. *The Athenian Agora* 1986

Davidson, J. *Courtesans and Fishcakes* 1997

De Sainte Croix, G. E. M. *Origins of the Peloponnesian War* 1972

Garland, R. *The Piraeus: From the Fifth to the First Century BC* 1988

Gill, D. 'Hippodamus and the Piraeus' *Historia* Bd. 55, H. 1, pp. 1–15 2006

Jankowski, C. *Hippocrates* 2007

Just, R. *Women in Athenian Law and Life* 1999

Matheson, S. B. *Polygnotus and Vase-Painting in Classical Athens* 1995

Matyszak, P. *Ancient Magic* 2019, and *Sparta: Fall of a Warrior Nation* 2018

Meiksins Wood, E. *Peasant-Citizen and Slave: The Foundations of Athenian Democracy* 1989

Morrison, J. S. & Coates J. F. *The Athenian Trireme* 1986

Osborne, R. *The World of Athens* 2008

Parke, H. W. *Festivals of the Athenians* Ithaca 1977

Parker, R. *Athenian Religion: A History* 1996

Robson, J. *Aristophanes: An Introduction* 2009

Santi Russell, F. *Information Gathering in Classical Greece* 2000

Signe, I & Skydsgaard. J. E. *Ancient Greek Agriculture: An Introduction* 1995.

Slater, W. J. (ed.) *Dining in a Classical Context* 1991

Ancient writers and texts quoted, referenced or plagiarized by the author

Homer
    Iliad 13
    Odyssey 122
Lucian
    On Pantomime 87
    Divine Dialogues 166
    Portrait Studies 196
    Dialogues of the Courtesans 166
Lycurgus, *Against Leocrates* 213
Lysias
    On the murder of Eratosthenes 123
    Against the Grain Dealers 211
Menander, *Methe* 97
Mine lease at Laurion 60
Old Oligarch, The 147
Orphic Hymn to Persephone 162
Papyri Graecae Magicae 79
Pausanias, *Guide to Greece* 41, 223
Plato
    Laws 90, 218
    Meno 23
    Phaedo 242
    Symposium 246, 247
Pliny the Elder, *Natural History* 22
Plutarch
    Alcibiades 125, 243
    Pericles 173, 196, 235
Polybius, *Histories* 14
Pseudo-Apollodorus, *Bibliotheca* 42
Sophocles fragment, 175
Tabulae Curatorum Navalium 50
Thucydides, *Peloponnesian War* 54, 58, 61, 223, 233

Index